CORNFIELD TO AIRFIELD:
A HISTORY OF COLUMBIA ARMY AIR BASE

Ed Benson shot the cover photo of **Lt. Col. Jimmy Doolittle** when the aviation pioneer and leader returned to Columbia, South Carolina June 19, 1942, on a morale tour. He had first been to CAAB in February that year to recruit crews for the audacious mission that went down in history as the Doolittle Raid. Benson had arrived at the airbase with the 17th Bombardment Group from Pendleton, Oregon.

CORNFIELD TO AIRFIELD: A HISTORY OF COLUMBIA ARMY AIR BASE

By **Rachel Haynie**
with
Primary Photography by **Bill Hamson**
U.S. Army Air Corps, retired

Commemorative Edition
70th Anniversary
Opening
Columbia Army Air Base
Columbia, South Carolina

E
Ellerbe Press

Ellerbe Press
801 King Street, Suite G
Columbia, South Carolina 29205

Copyright 2011 by Rachel Haynie
All Rights Reserved. Reproduction in whole or in part without
the express written permission of the author is prohibited.
info.EllerbePress@gmail.com

ISBN-13-978-1475032734
ISBN-10-1475032730

CORNFIELD TO AIRFIELD: A HISTORY OF COLUMBIA ARMY AIR BASE

Dedication

CORNFIELD TO AIRFIELD:
A HISTORY OF COLUMBIA ARMY AIR BASE

is
dedicated
to
the families of
Rachel Haynie
and
Bill and Mary Hamson
and
all families whose lives have been touched
by
Columbia Army Air Base
before, during and since its brief tenure as a military installation.

The insignia above was found on the service cap of Lt. Henry Mascall, navigator/bombardier trainer at Columbia Army Air Base. Mascall's cap was left in the cockpit of a B-25 when it ditched into Lake Murray early in April 1943. The Mitchell bomber had been on a routine training mission when it lost an engine. When that aircraft was recovered in Fall 2005 by the Lake Murray B-25 Rescue Group, the cap, which in those war years cost $17 to replace, was found in the debris, exactly where Mascall had left it. Image courtesy of Southern Museum of Flight, Birmingham, Alabama, where Lake Murray B-25 is on exhibition.

Acknowledgements

The stunning realization – that seven decades have flown by since the Imperial Japanese attack on Pearl Harbor, December 7, 1941, plunging the world deeper into war – has been shared by a number of individuals and institutions as a history of Columbia Army Air Base developed. News of the attack accelerated the scheduled opening of the Lexington County Airport. The undertaking was designed from the earliest stages as a commercial facility, but to also meet military specifications. The U.S. government's intention, in funding this complex – along with a network of other civilian locations situated strategically throughout the country – was to have available a viable aviation infrastructure should federal take over be made necessary by war.

Bill Hamson was part of Columbia Army Air Base's short history nearly from the beginning, documenting photographically both the hits and misses of bomb training missions.

He also photographed official activity on base: a continual cavalcade of top brass on site to review troops as well as an occasional celebrity. His personal collection of photographs from this by-gone era, so generously shared for publication of this book, includes shots he took around the sprawling base and, when he had even a little spare time to wander, in and around Columbia.

The Massachusetts native remained in the Columbia area following his military discharge to make a home, career and life. He married Mary Elinor Awtrey, a local girl who at the time of their introduction was a rising senior at Winthrop College. Their marriage ceremony followed Evening Vespers at Mt. Tabor Lutheran Church May 21, 1944. The couple has made Mt. Tabor its spiritual home all these years.

Hamson's astute attention for detail that served him so well as a photographer worked equally well in the business sector. After the war ended, he was offered a job with Columbia Lumber Company through an acquaintanceship forged at church. He remembered hand-hacking bark off the pine poles that held up the sign over his bomb squad's entrance and wondered if that qualified him for the job. He began in the lumber yard where no pine knot escaped his attention; he advanced through the ranks and retired from the local company in 1985 as vice president and general manager.

Ed Benson also was part of the photographic corps assigned to Columbia Army Air Base; his years of service overlapped those of William Hamson's, although the two don't remember each other. Every squadron had its own photographers – assigned to the same barracks, taking meals in the same mess halls as the rest of their squadrons. Benson shot the cover photograph for the book, and there are others within the pages from his collection. His generosity is greatly appreciated.

Harold Jones knows much of Columbia Army Air Base's history, formally and informally. Having grown up near the base, then establishing a business, some years after the war ended, on part of the former base, he knows the terrain well. He and Gary Smith founded Smith and Jones Antique Auto Parts in a former military building that remained on property that, in the late '40s, the government designated as surplus. On his own time, in his own vehicle using his own fuel, he has given countless informal tours of the former base, pointing out the few remnants still visible. He brokered the author's introduction to Bill Hamson. Jones identified countless others who have stories to tell about their ties to, and memories of, CAAB. In 2010 he discovered and refurbished the site where the base headquarters' flagpole stood during WWII, then led the charge to rededicate it in a patriotic flag-raising ceremony hosted December 5, 2010, by the South Carolina Historic Aviation Foundation. The community event also marked the 70th anniversary of the property's transfer from private farm owners to the federal government. In 1940 development began for the facility initially named Lexington County Airport; until The Day of Infamy (the attack on Pearl Harbor), the airport was projected to serve as a commercial enterprise. More recently, Jones has led a new charge: to find and compile names of more than 250 airmen who perished in training accidents while serving at CAAB. Plans are for those names to be etched into black granite and become the central element in a monument to the memory of those courageous airmen. The monument is to be designed, executed and installed by Memorial Design, Ron and Sallie Clamp of Stonecrafters Farm.

Dan Rossman, speaking from first hand experience about the air base, verified information and added new strands of thought to the research process for this book. For Rossman, being on Columbia Army Air Base for six weeks in the early spring of 1944 was a holding pattern. He was awaiting further orders which eventually sent him to Greenville AFB, another B-25 base that, for a time, had been a sub-base of CAAB. Flying out of Greenville AFB, he was piloting a B-25 that, records indicate, had been a CAAB aircraft earlier and then was on loan to Greenville. He was part of a full crew on a routine training mission on D-Day when the instructor pilot flew too close to the surface of Lake Greenwood, their training venue that day, when a wing tip touched the water, disabling the aircraft. The crew escaped, with some injuries; the plane sank. When he was cleared to return to duty, Rossman went on to distinguish himself as a pilot, logging 500 combat hours and numerous commendations. After being processed off active duty at the end of WWII, he continued flying with service in the Pennsylvania Air National Guard, then the Air Force Reserves. In retirement, he flies radio control planes near Roswell, Georgia.

Ron Shelton, science curator emeritus, South Carolina State Museum, has opened doors, traced informational leads and brokered introductions to individuals vital to the compilation of this information. He has assisted in fact checking and has suggested remedies for technological glitches. His encouragement has been unwavering. As he supported initiatives of the South Carolina Historic Aviation Foundation, of which he is a founding board member and vice president for outreach and education, he spearheaded events that served to promote this book by association.

Debra Bloom, Walker Local History Room Manager, Richland County Public Library, responded to the availability of Bill Hamson's scrapbook documenting his days at Columbia Army Air Base by offering to digitize them, thus making them available for use, not only for this book, but for other researchers. Bloom, along with Gene Sansbury and Margaret Dunlap, was instrumental in finding and documenting names of more than 250 servicemen who died in training mishaps while assigned to CAAB. Bloom has sought and offered myriad ways to be helpful in the advancement of this project, as she has and does for any effort that illuminates facets of Columbia's local history.

LaVonne Roof, along with Jeffrey and Carey Roof and other members of the extended Roof family, opened their scrapbooks and jogged their collective memories, dredging up factual details and lore about the farmers whose land transferred to the government after the South Carolina Aeronautics Commission recommended their acreage as the most desirable site in the area for development of an airport.

Valuable assistance also was given by Anna Amick, Dr. Robert Seigler, Dr. John Hammond Moore, Lynn Mascall Geis and Ed Geis, Jonna Doolittle Hoppes, Dave and Marty Sennema, David Suggs, Richard Peterson, Frances Addy Price, Murray Price, and Jerry Price, John Tokaz, and the board of the South Carolina Historic Aviation Foundation www.schistoricaviation.org. Archivists at Maxwell Air Force Base, the Air Force Historical Research Agency, provided invaluable information. Abundant thanks go to Pat Saad for her design insights and diligent effort.

CHAPTER ONE

This is a sad day for all of us, and to none is it sadder than to me. Everything that I have worked for, everything that I have believed in during my public life has crashed into ruins. There is only one thing left for me to do: That is, to devote what strength and powers I have to forwarding the victory of the cause for which we have to sacrifice so much... I trust I may live to see the day when Hitlerism has been destroyed and a liberated Europe has been re-established.

Neville Chamberlain
3rd September 1939

CHAPTER ONE

Rumblings of War

Months elapsed after Germany invaded unsuspecting Poland September 1, 1939; Great Britain and France had retaliated, taking Germany on in war, but United States President Franklin Delano Roosevelt continued saying America would be the "Arsenal of Democracy", but that this nation would not become involved in WWII.

Assistance for the Allies, in myriad forms, was forthcoming from America, though, so the nation was deeply involved behind the scenes – in many corners of the country. In March 1941 President Roosevelt signed the Lend-Lease Bill authorizing the U.S. to supply war materials to the United Kingdom, the Soviet Union, China, France and other Allied nations.

President Franklin Delano Roosevelt said American would not go to war but would be the "Arsenal of Democracy".

Training side by side at Woodward Field in Camden were airmen from Great Britain and America.

From June 1941 through 1945, Royal Air Force student pilots were being trained (alongside American pilots) in South Carolina, as close to Columbia as Camden, at Southern Aviation School headquartered at historic Woodward Field. In South Carolina's oldest inland city, airmen took their first sixty hours of flight instruction as part of a U.S. Army Air Forces Flying Training Detachment.

As a pro-active step – weighing odds that America could eventually be drawn into the war – the U.S. Department of Defense authorized the development of a grid of air strips, to be strategically located throughout the country. Congress appropriated a (then) staggering $40,000,000 for the development of 250 airports, then gave states a matter of only weeks to submit their site proposals, including cost estimates.

Any proposals considered would be for airfields that could be converted for military purposes quickly and efficiently if the need should arise, i.e., if America should be pulled into the war. That meant the facilities, to serve civilian purposes initially, had to meet military criteria – just in case.

The nation was still recoiling from The Great Depression; jobs still were scarce, money still tight, so the prospect of construction and other work to stimulate the local economy was promising to the public, even though war was the reason behind the potential – and sudden – availability of employment.

Columbia already knew the economic benefits of being a military town. In 1916 a group of civic leaders had proposed to Washington, D.C. officials that a base be located in the state capital. The announcement that Camp Jackson had been approved, and that an army cantonment would be established here, was made in May 1917 by Major Douglas MacArthur.

The local chamber of commerce led the campaign to raise $50,000 to purchase acreage held within the Hampton estate, amassed by three genera-

Property that went into the development of Fort Jackson came from the estate of three generations of South Carolina leaders, all named Wade Hampton. Adjacent to the Wade Hampton state office building is a statue to one of them.
Photograph by Bill Hamson

tions of leaders named Wade Hampton. Residents donated 1,992 acres and the federal government purchased 19,700 additional acres for initial development of the army base. Before the outbreak of WWII, the name changed to Fort Jackson and the base expanded to 53,000 acres.

The identification of plausible airport sites within South Carolina fell to the state's first aeronautic's commissioner; the aeronautics commission (SCAC) had been established in 1935. Dexter C. Martin had toured the southeast with Mabel Cody's famous Flying Circus. His initial pilot's license had been signed by Orville Wright in 1919, and in 1924 he became the first licensed pilot in South Carolina. From his years as a barnstormer, he knew a good place for landing and taking off when he saw one, but this decision would require more than an aerial glance. There were many considerations to be made – in short order.

Well aware that his state's recommendations had to be filed in Washington, D.C. no later than 13 November 1940, Martin pulled together a search committee comprised of his own commission members, plus municipal and county officials to help him inspect possible sites in and around Columbia and throughout the rest of the state.

Their mission was to find property characterized by evenness of terrain, good drainage, proximity to Columbia, freedom from any obstructions that might compromise or endanger instrument flying, and freedom also from smoke in the air near the airport. A tract of land that held the potential for later expansion also factored into the difficult equation.

The search team's attention ultimately rested upon land featuring a small knoll between two drainage basins, generally on a plateau at an elevation of approximately 235 feet. The site was noted because of its elevation, the nature of its terrain, and the area's good soil, believed to be favorable for the construction of landing facilities such as taxiways, aprons, and runways.

But when the commission search team found what they believed to be the best possible location for their recommendation, they met with resistance.

Unlike during WWI when Columbians rallied around a civic campaign to attract a military base in northeast Richland County, sentiment was lacking when late in 1940 long-held family property, being actively farmed, was pinpointed as the most promising place for developing an air field in the state's midlands.

Located approximately six miles southwest of the City of Columbia were contiguous tracts of fertile land that, for generations, had been cultivated by local families. When those land owners first received overtures that revealed the committee's interest in offering the property for defense purposes, they had just stored their corn to feed their cattle and livestock through the winter. They had just baled the last of the cotton from that season's harvest. It was hog killing time; collards in their truck gardens were ready for pulling, and sweet potatoes awaiting digging.

As real estate negotiations began, the Lexington County legislative delegation passed a resolution to acquire the land and committed to allocating funds to develop it. Meanwhile, the SCAC contracted with four engineering firms to survey the designated Lexington County site. To factor into the budgetary component of the proposal for the defense department were solid estimates as to how much earth would have to be moved, where property lines were located, in addition to information needed to prepare maps and charts.

Planners in South Carolina submitted proposals for construction of three principle runways, with acreage available for additional runways to be undertaken later under the expansion program. Clearing, draining, grading of the entire area – 600 acres – would have to take place, and all would have to be fenced and equipped with lighting facilities. In the initial proposal, planners projected five hangar sites and an administration building.

Fortunately, South Carolina was not the only state having trouble meeting the very short time frame the department of defense initially set. A blanket one week extension was granted. Martin and members of the planning team flew South Carolina's proposal package to Washington, D.C. to assure the state's submission was placed personally into the right hands on November 20, the new deadline.

Almost before the commission and others involved in the proposal process could catch their collective breath following the whirlwind process and delivery, Washington was ready with an answer. On 12 December South Carolina was notified the Lexington County project had received approval, along with $562,000 that could be applied to immediate construction start-up. However, there were to be revisions, so the momentum stalled temporarily.

Of the sum awarded, an initial grant of $31,900 was allocated for development of the eventual landing facilities: paved runways and taxi strips. This initial appropriation only provided funding enough for the paving of two runways. The north-south runway was to be paved with a strip 4,500 feet long and 600 feet wide. The east-west runway was to be 3,000 feet long and 100 feet wide. Five hangar sites and an administration building also were calculated into that initial plan.

The remainder, $243,000, was to be used in construction of buildings for occupancy of military personnel to be stationed at the field.

The South Carolina delegation also learned that additional appropriations could be forthcoming for expansions that ultimately would render the new field a "super" airport, capable of accommodating several squadrons of the Army Air Corps.

Working out details to reflect the revisions called for in the federal government's approval of the proposal delayed until 5 April, 1941 the announcement that bids were then open. By end of May that year, C.C. Fuller of Barnwell, South Carolina, came in at the lowest bid – $633,895. Construction began one month later, with the project under the supervision of the U.S. Corps of Engineers, Charleston District. Estimates were that the project would be completed by 1 February 1942; however, weather and other natural causes delayed efforts sporadically.

The balance of powers in national-local partnership teetered when lack of water threatened to jeopardize the project. The war department dug in its heels, stating it was not responsible for supplying water to the construction site, that laying the water main was not authorized as an expenditure as a national defense measure. After more delays Lexington County found the funds for the laying of the water main within funding for a WPA project and came up with $54,000 to lay about five miles of eighty-inch water main in order to hook onto the West Columbia lines.

Even while under construction, the airport had been in use by the 105th Observation Squadron flying light observation aircraft, Douglas O-38s and North American O-47s from 24 September 1941.

On 2 December 1941, Major Charles Gableman, the project engineer, announced the work was ninety-eight percent complete. Ready for use and occupancy were the two paved runways, one hangar, one water tower, ten wooden office buildings, some sleeping quarters, messes and latrines. For the time being, military personnel would be housed in tents.

CHAPTER TWO

```
F L A S H

    WASHINGTON--WHITE HOUSE SAYS JAPS ATTACK PEARL HARBOR.

                                                        222PES




B U L L E T I N


    WASHINGTON, DEC. 7 (AP)-PRESIDENT ROOSEVELT SAID IN A
STATEMENT TODAY THAT THE JAPANESE HAD ATTACKED PEARL HARBOR, HAWAII,
FROM THE AIR.
    THE ATTACK OF THE JAPANESE ALSO WAS MADE ON ALL NAVAL AND MILITARY
"ACTIVITIES" ON THE ISLAND OF OAHU.
    THE PRESIDENT'S BRIEF STATEMENT WAS READ TO REPORTERS BY STEPHEN
EARLY, PRESIDENTIAL SECRETARY. NO FURTHER DETAILS WERE GIVEN
IMMEDIATELY.
    AT THE TIME OF THE WHITE HOUSE ANNOUNCEMENT, THE JAPANESE AMBASSADO
KIURISABORO NOMURA AND SABURO KURUSU, WERE AT THE STATE DEPARTMENT.




F L A S H
        WASHINGTON--SECOND AIR ATTACK REPORTED ON ARMY AND NAVY BASES
IN MANILA.
```

Never in the field of human conflict, has so much been owed by so many to so few!

Winston Churchill
September 1940

CHAPTER TWO

Pearl Harbor

On Sunday morning, December 7, 1941, the Imperial Japanese Navy attacked the US naval station at Pearl Harbor, home of the Pacific Fleet.

In two waves six Japanese aircraft carriers launched 350 fighters and bombers sinking, beaching or damaging twelve ships, demolishing 164 American aircraft and damaging another 159. Killed were 2,340 US military personnel, about half of whom died on the battleship Arizona, as well as Marine Corps and Army air and ground bases, along with civilians. Wounded were 1,143 servicemen and 35 civilians.

America still was reeling from that unprovoked assault when Germany and Italy declared war on the US. Japan invaded British colonies Hong Kong and Malaya. American territories Guam and the Philippines also fell, then the Asian warmongers continued their devastating swath.

Meanwhile, German U-boats sank 216 ships, mostly tankers, along the unprepared American Atlantic and Gulf coasts, close enough to shore that American citizens often witnessed the ships burning.

American's spirit was at a historic low. While it seemed the nation was sitting on its collective hands, glued to the radio and to newspapers, dreading what might unfold next, retribution was being planned.

Immediately following the assault on Hawaii, President Franklin D. Roosevelt had begun pressing his chiefs of staff for a plan to avenge the costly and unprecedented strike. On January 10, 1942 Captain Francis S. "Frog" Low, a submariner on the staff of Admiral Ernest J. King, had flown to Norfolk, Virginia, to assess the readiness of the US Navy's newest aircraft carrier.

As the plane on which he was aboard for his return flight to Washington, D.C. banked on take-off, he noticed from his window a white outline on one of the runways. Painted onto the asphalt were the dimensions of an aircraft carrier. Navy pilots were using the outline as guidelines and parameters for their take-offs and landings from the carrier.

That sight triggered a thought, and it flashed through the captain's mind. Would it be possible for a USAAF medium bomber to take off from an aircraft carrier? If so, the medium bomber's capability for longer range could ostensibly accommodate a launch from a safe distance out at sea, out of the Imperial Navy's reach.

As soon as Low returned to Washington, he took his idea straightaway to Admiral King who ordered his top air officer to study the idea, troubleshoot it if it struck him as plausible. Five days later Captain Donald B. "Wu" Duncan delivered his 30-page analysis, detailed in handwriting (for security reasons). As soon as the admiral reviewed it, he sent both Low and Duncan to present the concept to General Henry H. "Hap" Arnold.

The two presenters had barely made it to the elevator before Arnold had sent for the man he felt was ideal to evaluate such a radical proposal. His trouble-shooter was Lt. Colonel James H. Doolittle.

No wonder it was Doolittle that Arnold sent for when the question had to be: "Jim, what bomber do we have that will get off in 500 feet with a 2,000 pound bomb load, then fly 2,000 miles?"

Doolittle had traveled the nation during the previous two decades as a star of both air racing and the U.S. Aerobatics Team. He had set many records

Photo by Bill Hamson

and broken some of his own, tested troubled aircraft, surveyed England's besieged aviation industry, and helped American auto industry manufacturers convert their lines so as to produce plane engines and assemble aircraft.

In only one day Doolittle studied the question and come back with an answer. At that follow-up meeting with "Hap" Arnold, the conundrum took on yet another requirement: the aircraft must take off within the narrow width of 75 feet. With that condition added to the mix, there was but one correct answer: the 67-foot wingspan B-25. The B-25B was chosen over the Martin B-26 for this mission because of its superior take-off performance.

When Doolittle heard the tenets of the proposed secret retaliation, he volunteered to head the initiative, see that the necessary planes were modified to specifications, and train the crews.

Arnold accepted Doolittle's offer, but he had no intentions that the man heading the effort would take the leading role as pilot, pathfinder.

While Washington made highly secret overtures to both Nationalist China and the Soviet Union asking permission to land aircraft in their territories – and recoiled from rejections both countries gave – Doolittle was flying back and forth between the nation's capital, Wright Field, and the Minneapolis shop in which Mid-Continent Airlines was setting up to modify the B-25s that would make the audacious flight.

By January 22 18 B-25s left Wright Field for the Minneapolis shop. B-25 modifications for this top-secret project involved removing the lower gun turret, saving some 600 lbs. in weight, and installing 50-gallon fuel tanks in its place, bringing the total internal fuel capacity to 1141 gallons, nearly doubling the normal 694 gallons. Additionally, five-gallon cans were to be carried in the airplane.

Special low-level bomb sights were built as the bombing altitude for this mission was to top out at only 1500 feet. Such an alternative also avoided use of the Norden bombsight which safeguarded one of WWII's top secrets from the possibility of falling into enemy hands.

To discourage the enemy from making tail attacks, broomsticks – painted black – were installed in the extreme rear fuselage in the position usually occupied by .50-cal guns.

Although modifications continued right down to take-off, most were accomplished in February, 1942 in Minnesota.

At the time of the Pearl Harbor attack, the nearest B-25s were stationed along the Pacific Coast. Immediately after the Day of Infamy, the 34th,

37th, and 95th Squadrons, which comprised the 17th Bombardment Group (Medium), were diverted to anti-submarine patrols along the Pacific Coast, assignments that capitalized upon their bomb load and long range. Their vigilance had been ordered in response to the December 7, 1941, attack.

Across the continent from Washington, D.C. and Columbia, South Carolina, airmen of the 17th Bombardment Group added daily to their B-25 flying experience by taking off from Pendleton Air Field and running patrols off the coasts of Oregon and Washington.

Early in February, the base commander at the Lexington County Airport was alerted to prepare for the reception of the 17th Bombardment Group arriving from Pendleton, Oregon, to serve in the newly-activated Eighth Air Force.

When the crews received orders to report to Lexington County Airport in Columbia, South Carolina, they figured their patrols were simply switching coasts. Welcoming the opportunity to evade the northwestern winter, hopefully to partake of some Southern cooking and meet some Southern Belles, they were happy to fly their planes across country.

When a few of the planes were ordered to stop over in Minneapolis en route to Columbia, questions began spreading among the squadron: what could be up?

Photo by Bill Hamson

CHAPTER THREE

Photo by Bill Hamson

Yesterday, December 7, 1941 - a date which will live in infamy - The United States of America was suddenly and deliberately attacked by naval and air forces of the Empire of Japan...As Commander-in-Chief of the Army and Navy, I have directed that all measures be taken for our defense...With confidence in our armed forces - with the unbounded determination of our people - we will gain the inevitable triumph - so help us God.

President F.D. Roosevelt
8th December 1941

CHAPTER THREE

Ramping Up

The new airport had barely been usable when, on 8 December 1941 Lt. Colonel Daches Reeves took command of the base. Under his command was the 65th Observation Group, comprised of the 105th and 112th Observations Squadrons, attached to the First Army Corps. A unit of the Tennessee National Guard temporarily had been stationed nearby at Owens Field, so the relocation to the new airport was made promptly, but not for long. Reeves and the observations personnel were ordered to report to Langley AFB in Virginia, on Christmas Day. Captain John J. Kennedy assumed command of the new base on a temporary basis due to the illness and hospitalization of Colonel William B. Mayer.

The first enlisted personnel to report for duty on the base came from the infantry at Fort Jackson. Master Sergeant Harrington, acting as First Sergeant, wrote his observations:

"At that time there was nothing here but sand and scrubbed pine growth, with the exception that a North and South runway had been completed, and the present hangar building was two-thirds completed."

But from that point, personnel and equipment were transferred to the Lexington base so that formation of a bombardment group could commence.

From 25 December until about mid-February 1942, the base still was under survey by the Flying Training Command, Air Services Command and various other departments to settle upon the best use for the base. After weighing all determinates, decision makers concluded Lexington County Airport would serve as a bombardment station. Whether proximity to Lake Murray was part of their deliberation is not known.

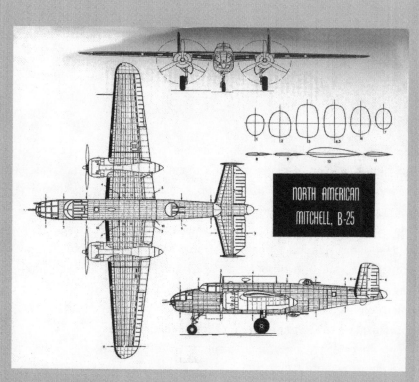

The B-25

The B-25's original design, as accepted by the Army Air Corps, called for a high-speed mid-wing monoplane powered by two 1650-hp Wright Cyclones with superchargers, driving constant-speed Hamilton Standard Hydromatic three-bladed propellers of 12-ft., 7-in. diameter. The bomb load was calculated. The design was planned for a crew of five: pilot, co-pilot, bombardier, radio operator and gunner. Access to the nose was by a tunnel under the pilot, and to the rear by way of a crawlway over the bomb-bay.

Considered a supreme achievement by its manufacturer, North American Aviation, Inc., the plane was manufactured in Inglewood, California, and flight-tested at Wright Field, Ohio, and became a favorite with almost every air crew assigned to it. Although it was characteristically loud, it was known to be a docile, adaptable, operationally efficient airplane with excellent all-round performance and particularly good handling characteristics.

The B-25 was manufactured in greater quantities than any other American twin-engined bomber; close to 10,000 were built. Of those, most went to Allied air forces; with Allied air crews, this plane was one of the most popular American-supplied types.

No other medium bomber underwent as many modifications, both in the factory and under field conditions – sometimes in primitive circumstances. The aircraft's simple but rugged structure and somewhat flat lines allowed maximum modifications made with a minimum of tools at advanced combat bases, giving the B-25 great versatility.

Dollar for dollar, the B-25 returned more productive value than almost any other plane.

The B-25 served in all WWII's principle war zones, playing a sizable role in smashing Rommel's Afrika Korps. It aided in the great Russian winter offensive, shot and bombed its way through the Pacific, and saw combat in Alaska, the Mediterranean, Europe, Burma, the American shoreline.

By the end of B-25 production, more than 900 subcontractors had been involved in manufacturing North American Aviation, Inc.'s design. Fisher Body Division of General Motors was the biggest provider of subassemblies.

If it had no greater claim to fame than that it was the first airplane by which the Americans took the war back to the enemy in the famous Doolittle raid on Tokyo, it would still have been a great airplane.

Background

The threat of actual incidence of war was heating up in Europe early in 1939, and on January 25, the Army Air Corps sent out invitations to manufacturers asking for design data submissions for a medium bombardment airplane that would replace the Douglas B-18 bombers that had become obsolete.

North American Aviation, Inc.'s proposal was one of two bombers selected for production. The Inglewood, California-based company named the bomber Mitchell to honor Brigadier General William "Billy" Mitchell, who in the 1920s prophesied the great importance air power would have in future national defense.

On September 1, 1939, just 19 days prior to the Army's contract for the B-25, war broke out in Europe and the Nazi's air power catalyzed North American Aviation's urgency of manufacturing, emphasizing ease and rapidity of manufacturing made possible by a plan that allowed hundreds of suppliers and subcontractors to furnish equipment and subassemblies, originally in 48 major component sections.

Fisher Body Division of General Motors was the biggest provider of subassemblies

By the end of B-25 production, some 921 subcontractors had been involved.

Leo J. Kohn, in an overview for the pilot's manual, described the aircraft as a "docile, adaptable, operationally efficient airplane with excellent all-round performance and particularly good handling characteristics."

Off the North American Aviation, Inc. assembly line came 9,812 aircraft, manufactured in greater quantities than any other American twin-engine bomber, at the factory or under primitive field conditions. This B-25 also was modified more than others; tts simple yet rugged structure allowed for changes, some in factories, many in the field.

Service

From smashing Rommel's Afrika Korps to aiding in the great Russian winter offensive, the B-25 Mitchell served all principal WWII war zones – including combat in Alaska, the Mediterranean, Europe, Burma, the American shorelines, and – in a later timeframe – Korea.

Early in April 1942, 10 B-25s equipped with auxiliary fuel tanks accompanied three B-17s from Darwin, Australia to the Philippines where, operating out of clandestine airstrips, they raided Japanese-held docks, air and harbor facilities and other military targets.

For one single action in the Bismark Sea, every available B-25 in the Pacific area was modified quickly to perform special missions. The result was the Fifth Air Force units' successful attack and destruction of 10 warships, 12 transports or merchant vessels, 61 enemy aircraft, and the loss of 12,700 Japanese officers and men, equivalent to a full division.

B-25s of the 3rd Bombardment Group also began operations in early April YEAR against targets in New Guinea, and after that, the aircraft's role in warfare increased.

Allies and the B-25

Under Lend-Lease, the agreement signed March 11, 1941 under which the United States supplied the United Kingdom, the Soviet Union, China, France, and other Allies with materials needed for defense, Russian pilots were sent to the United States late in 1941 for training in B-25s, aircraft also were supplied.

The British Air Ministry received 23 B-25Bs which were used for familiarization and training, those aircraft never reaching operational status. The Royal Air Force received 433 B-25Cs; their first action took place January 22, 1943 with a raid on Belgium oil refineries.

For the Netherlands East Indies Air Force, 162 B-25C-5_NA were manufactured, the Defense Aid for China.

B-25C

Initially, the Army reordered 863 B-25s in an improved version designated at Cs. The B-25C was basically unchanged from the B-25B used in the Tokyo raid, including the same autopilots, and the installation of Wright R-2600-13 engines.

In addition to previous modifications, the manufacturer added external bomb racks, an additional .50-calibre fixed gun in the nose, and a flexible .50-calibre gun substituted for the .30-calibre weapon. Self-sealing oil and gas tanks and a larger escape hatch, upgraded radio equipment, superchargers and armor plate.

Photo by Bill Hamson

CHAPTER FOUR

Photo by Bill Hamson

There is nothing stronger than the heart of a volunteer.

> (Then) Lt. Colonel Jimmy Doolittle

CHAPTER FOUR

Volunteers, All

The men destined to become Doolittle Raiders belonged to the 17th Bombardment Group (Medium) which, from June 1941 until February 1942, was based at Pendleton Field, Oregon.

While Washington was scurrying in secret to cobble together components for the daring mission that would rain furry on the Imperial Japanese in retaliation for that its unprovoked attack on Pearl Harbor a few months earlier, Lexington County Airport was being readied to play its role in an historic episode.

Daniel Peterson, an OSS officer, was sent to Columbia, soon after his commissioning to begin screening airmen for the highly-secret mission that would go down in history as the Doolittle Raid.

The men of the 17th were stunned when Lt. Col. Jimmy Doolittle strode into the hangar for a briefing they had been called to. For many of the airmen recently arriving in Columbia from Pendleton, Oregon, Doolittle was the inspiration behind their wanting to fly. He was their hero, their role model.

During the two previous decades when most of the airmen were growing up – in the 1920s and '30s, – Doolittle had starred in US Army aerobatics as well as air racing,

Dan Peterson came to CAAB to screen volunteers for what became the Doolittle Raid.
Courtesy Richard Peterson

25

sponsored by corporations as a means of showcasing their products and services. He had distinguished himself in this and other hemispheres by pulling out of seemingly death-defying stunts that pushed the envelope on aeronautic science. Throughout the world he was among a small number to hold advanced degrees in Aeronautical Engineering; his was a Ph.D. from Massachusetts Institute of Technology.

As early as 1922, he had been the first pilot to fly across the country in under 24 hours. Nine years later he was first again, this time he accomplished that cross-country feat in under 12 hours. Between those two pioneering achievements – in 1927 – he executed the first outside loop.

But perhaps his greatest contribution to the advancement of aeronautical science during that era was in instrument development and flying. In 1929 he made the first blind flight into history, using only instruments. In his cockpit the windows were hooded.

Between 1925 and 1932, he won the "Big Three" in air racing. At the 1925 Schneider Trophy Race at Chesapeake Bay, he established a world speed record. In the 1931 Bendix Trophy Race, he added his next transcontinental triumph. The following year he set another record in the infamous Bee Gee; in the aircraft considered by many a flying death trap, he took the Thompson trophy at the National Air Races.

His prowess brought him to the attention of Shell Oil Company, and when they offered, he accepted a job managing its Aviation department, where he experimented with high-octane fuels. He had resigned his regular Army commission in 1920, continuing on reserve status. When war in Europe broke out in 1939, he returned to uniform at the rank of major.

Once back on active duty in 1940, his first Army Air Corps mission was to help auto industries convert plants to produce plane engines and assemble aircraft. The following year as war spread, the new Army Air Forces sent him to England to survey the United Kingdom's aviation industry.

His multi-faceted experience with aircraft, flying, and the business that fueled each made him the ideal individual to take on the challenge of reciprocating, on America's behalf, for the horrific harm the Japanese had caused.

Jimmy Doolittle in his early flying years.
From StockExchange.com

CHAPTER FIVE

Photo by Ed Benson

Our citizens can now rejoice that a momentous victory is in the making. Perhaps we will be forgiven if we claim we are about midway to our objective.

Admiral Chester Nimitz
June 1942

CHAPTER FIVE

1942

The base was just beginning to take shape, although the cantonment was still a tent city and there was not yet a hospital. But many improvements were on the drawing board, and once a project was approved, it was carried out with haste and efficiency.

Early in February, the base commander at the Lexington County Airport was alerted to prepare for the reception of the 17th Bombardment Group comprised of the 34th, 37th, and 95 bomb squads, arriving from Pendleton, Oregon, to comprise the newly-activated Eighth Air Force.

On 6 February 1942 the first medical-department personnel to be stationed at the base arrived from Hunter Field, Savannah, Georgia, and began

Courtesy South Caroliniana Library

setting up a temporary dispensary. All hospital patients were evacuated to Fort Jackson. By 25 February, a Base Surgeon had been assigned.

The Dispensary.
Photo by Bill Hamson

The first group to be equipped by the Base Quartermaster was the 21st Bombardment Group (Medium) which arrived in late April 1942. The quartermaster was able to issue approximately 3,100 cots, mattresses, pillows and other bedding items, all of which were stored in tents.

To accommodate the influx of personnel arriving, 150 buildings were hastily constructed. Personnel less likely to be shipped overseas on short notice were allowed to find accommodations in town.

During spring and summer of 1942, countless projects required the attention of the base engineer. One was the coal coating of the runways, an initiative that could not be completed earlier, in part because the area to be hard-surfaced had so recently been open farmland, portions of which contained sand to a depth of between twenty-five and fifty feet. Below the sand was a stratum of kaolin which formed an impervious layer and controlled the water table. Drainage was such a problem that some kaolin deposits had to be replaced with a porous stabilizing material in order to prepare strips capable of receiving the weight of the B-25s. Ultimately, runways were paved with sand asphalt to thicknesses of five inches.

Another project checked off that quarter was night lighting for the entire base. The contract for this project had been awarded in early July 1941 when the airport was under construction; however, materials were back-ordered and supplies were delayed as supplies for the war effort were priorities.

On 13 April 1942 Col. Gilbert Collar assumed command of the base, and two days later, the first combat group to complete training at the base moved out. In this group were airmen not chosen for the highly secret mission Doolittle had recruited for in early February.

From the time the 17th Bomb Squadron arrived at the Lexington base, its men and experience had contributed to the development of all other groups assigned there. They were considered the parent group and were nicknamed "The Daddy of Them All."

The first entertainment band was organized on base 13 June 1942. Comprised of combat personnel, which meant its complement varied from day to day, from orders to orders, the group provided music for dances and informal entertainment.

The first in a series of morale boosts stemming from the band's organization came about a month later when on 14 July 1942 the first dance was held on base. Musicians set up just outside the Finance Office on the bed of one of the crash trucks and, with improvised lighting and few decorations, made the occasion memorable for base personnel.

Throughout the summer of 1942 dust storms over the airfield impaired flying Although the installation of turf helped in many areas, the critical spaces between the flying line and the adjacent runways defied stabilization until authorization was attained to replace loose topsoil with six-inch soil-cement base sealed with tar prime.

Since work was being done on the runways, approval was obtained to replace the original paving, which consisted of sand asphalt on prepared sub-base, with concrete paving.

Courtesy Frances Addy Price

Photo by Bill Hamson

Also that summer Walterboro's Anderson Airport became the first sub-base of Columbia Army Air Base. By summer's end Greenwood and Congaree had become sub-bases as well, although Greenwood was changed to an auxiliary field a few months later. Soon after, Aiken, South Carolina, was added as a sub-base, and North became an auxiliary field.

Numerous bombardment groups were activated at CAAB later that summer and in early fall. In time, the base emerged as one of the Allies' largest B-25 training center. Wherever B-25s were in the air heading to or back from medium altitude targets, they quite likely were being crewed by airmen cleared for combat at the Lexington County base.

On 10 August 1942, the Air Force Band was activated and re-designated a few days later as the 61st Army Air Forces Band. Besides its contributions to base morale, the band furnished music for military formations.

By late September a new dance band, drawing its musicians from the Air Base Band and calling itself the "Jive Bombers", emerged on base, but provided entertainment off base as well, especially at weekly dances in Lexington and at the USO in Columbia.

Shortly before the first anniversary of the Pearl Harbor attack, the official band participated in Lexington ceremonies honoring the heroes of December 7, 1941. Just before Christmas the band rallied around to dedicate the flagpole at base headquarters.

The base integrated on 29 October 1941 when the 339th Squadron (colored) was activated.

The pace at which the base grew made it impossible for construction to keep up, and understandably, building materials were hard to come by, so in November 1942 Civilian Conservation Buildings from other sites were dismantled and moved to CAAB. Six buildings from Lexington Camp were re-erected, then twelve from Bradley Camp and twenty-six from Ninety-Six Camp. These were used for special training activities as well as recreation facilities. Repurposing buildings from other sites for these non-housing or regular training functions was a frugal approach to using resources in ways that did not compromise the overall development of the base nor deplete supplies needed for the war effort.

New hospital buildings were occupied on 22 November 1942, and by then work already had begun on the Flight Surgeon's office where care could be administered to flying personnel arriving steadily.

Christmas Day 1942 was celebrated on base in the company of seventy-five orphans from Epworth Children's Home on Millwood Avenue in Columbia. Many of the gifts the children received had been made in the craft shop on base, frequented by both hail and hardy servicemen as well as those convalescing in the hospital.

CAAB servicemen host residents of Epworth Children's Home at Christmas.
Photo by Bill Hamson

Photo by Bill Hamson

At the end of 1942, total personnel on base, exclusive of the bombardment training groups, included approximately one thousand officers and enlisted men. Under the base's jurisdiction were three sub-bases: Walterboro, Congaree, and Aiken, as well as three military fields: in Greenwood, Barnwell, and North. Steps toward establishment of an Altitude Training Unit were underway along with construction of buildings to be used in celestial navigation training.

Photo by Bill Hamson

CHAPTER SIX

Photo by Bill Hamson

Before we're through with them, the Japanese language will be spoken only in hell.

> Admiral Halsey
> December 1941

CHAPTER SIX

White Lines! Why?

Rumors, then the proof that Doolittle – in the flesh – was, or had been on base, ratcheted up the esprit de corps at every rank – and spread even to civilians working in myriad capacities.

Russell Maxey was among those who wasn't military. As part of the U.S. Corps of Engineers, he had been on the base since its early development.

Doolittle was no where to be seen when Maxey received orders to paint white lines on the brand new runway – to very specific dimensions.

Maxey wasn't military, although he was an engineer with the U.S. Corps of Engineers, so he obeyed the base commander's orders nevertheless. Scuttlebutt was that orders to paint the white outline had come directly from Lt. Col James Doolittle.

The colonel had no official standing on the base, but his reputation as a fearless flyer and compelling leader inspired Maxey to comply, without questions. Maxey knew for a fact Doolittle had been on the base the day before, adding credence to the rumor that the mysterious orders had come down through the chain of command, starting with the renowned aviator.

Maxey had been on the airfield project from its 1940 inception. Along with 49 other engineers with the U.S. Corps of Engineers and hundreds of civilians, he had been on the clock nearly non-stop to convert scruffy, but fairly level, woods and agricultural fields into a county airport.

The Columbia native had complied with the order to paint the white lines. To make sure they were dry, he returned to the runway, following unnatural engine sounds. As he approached the runway, he witnessed something baffling.

There, straining against the power of an earth mover that, earlier in the day, had smoothed layers of soil and concrete onto the third and last runway, a B-25 groaned at the end of rope. Just when the plane had stretched the tether to its absolute tensile capacity, the rope was cut and the craft lofted almost straight up. Maxey whipped off his cap and scratched his head. What did his hero Doolittle, the aeronautical mastermind, think would be accomplished by such training?

His answer was weeks in the offing.

For the remainder of February, airmen practiced short-runs, lifting off before reaching the lines Maxey had painted, but they still couldn't guess what mission could be important enough for Jimmy Doolittle himself to be giving the orders. Paint from the white lines had begun to chip off, helped along by late winter rains, when new orders swept through the base. By March 1 airmen not chosen for the mission were back to flying anti-submarine patrols off the Atlantic coast, and training new arrivees at the Lexington base. Those, from the willing volunteers, who had been chosen for the Doolittle's mission, were off to continue training in secret.

Photo by Bill Hamson

CHAPTER SEVEN

Photo by Bill Hamson

Our losses...have reached an intolerable level. The enemy air force played a decisive role in inflicting these high losses.

> Grand Admiral Carl Donitz
> Commander-in-Chief of the German Navy
> 24th May 1943

CHAPTER SEVEN
Florida – Not much of a spring break

Once the crews chosen for the top-secret mission took off from the Lexington County Airport, there still was connectivity. One particularly talented mechanic commuted back and forth, making adjustments, bringing parts, even ferrying a plane to the new training location.

Photo by Bill Hamson

Eglin Air Force Base, just outside Pensacola, Florida, was the U.S. Army Air Corps' proving ground, with seven or eight fields away from the main strips where airmen demonstrated they could take off and land in a mosquito-infested swamp without rousing the curiosity of the citizenry.

Crews thought surely they would get some time to relax on the wide white beaches just across the highways, and a few did pay – with goose bumps – for an early swim in the Gulf of Mexico, but their training regimen demanded most of their time.

A different kind of pay-off came in early March when Doolittle showed up again. They knew he had been the mastermind of the mission; now he told them he also would be leading it. Although he had been told in Washington he was too valued as a staff member to take the risk, he nevertheless secured this authorization with an end run: by talking fast and moving quickly to seal off permission on the other end.

In his briefings with the chosen crews, Doolittle was forthright. "It is inevitable that some of the ships will fall into enemy hands." Unwilling to presume every American serviceman calculated risk as astutely as he did, he offered again an easy out to anyone who wanted one. There were no takers. Doolittle stressed again the need for utmost secrecy. "If anybody outside this group gets nosy, get his name and give it to me; the FBI will find out all about him."

Photo by Bill Hamson

CHAPTER EIGHT

On the deck of the Hornet.
Courtesy Martin Crouch

Victory belongs to those who believe in it the most and believe in it the longest. We're gonna' believe. We're gonna' make Americans believe, too.

(Then) Lt. Colonel Jimmy Doolittle

CHAPTER EIGHT

Return to West Coast, then to sea

Before March elapsed and long before they could work on suntans, the crews were ordered to McClellan Air Force Base near Sacramento, Calif., where they continued training as secretly as possible, including runway work at a nearby airstrip, Willows, and last minute engine adjustments at the Sacramento Air Depot.

They quickly moved down coast to Alameda where the B-25s were hoisted onto the deck of the USS Hornet, positioned closely, tied down for safety and tarped for security. Once again, painted lines were precursors to the making of history.

The Hornet, in convoy with Task Force 16, comprised of Vice Admiral William Halsey's carrier, the USS Enterprise, a fuel tanker, escort cruisers and destroyers, had steamed to within 100 miles of their strategic launch point. White lines were painted, this time to mark where both the left wheel and nose wheel should set, leaving six feet as insurance. Each bomber carried two 500 pound demolition bombs, to be followed by a 1,000 pound incendiary bomb.

In a motivational ceremony, Japanese "friendship" medals were affixed to the tips of some of the bombs. The tokens were given American military personnel only months before Japan bombed Pearl Harbor. As Doolittle attached the first one, a roar of naval and army patriotic thunder followed his grinning announcement: "Your government has asked that you politely return these."

Final briefings were given, the planes had been rocked to rid gas tanks of bubbles, and the ship's doctor had issued each crew two pints of medicinal rye, emphasizing the whiskey's antiseptic qualities. Expecting they'd be taking off in 10 hours, the crew had stowed in their bags items not likely available in China: razor blades, toothpaste, candy bars, and cigarettes.

Warned about China's primitive sanitation, Columbia's Horace "Sally" Crouch stashed rolls of toilet paper in his bag. Another airman insisted on taking his wind-up phonograph with him; his plane was fully packed when he realized his cake tin of records hadn't been stowed, so he pleaded with a buddy to secure his treasure under the crew seat of his plane.

Absent from all bags were personal items that could tie a crewman with any base on which he'd served, any place he'd been, anyone he loved. Diaries, journals, and photographs were secured in a box to be returned to stateside later.

The planned take-off was timed to position the planes over Tokyo after nightfall. That schedule gave the crew one more chance for some sleep. Suddenly, a Japanese picket boat, disguised as a fishing boat, appeared in the scope of a crewman on watch. That the task force had been spotted was confirmed immediately when a Japanese radio message was intercepted and interpreted. Roiling waves and pea-soup visibility delayed for nine full minutes the USS Nashville's sinking of Nitto Maru.

So, ten hours earlier than planned and 170 miles farther out than fuel had been calculated and allocated, the Hornet's klaxon blared: "Army pilots, man your planes!" and 16 B-25s took off for Tokyo.

It was the first and only time Army Air Force bombers launched for a combat mission from a Navy carrier.

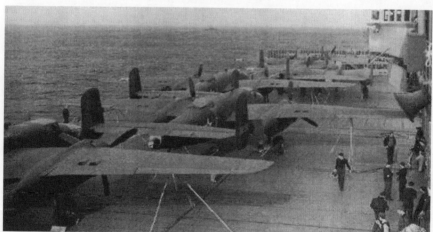

B-25s were tightly aligned on the deck of the USS Hornet awaiting orders to take off for the raid on Tokyo.
Courtesy Martin Crouch

Throughout a three hour offensive, targets hit in broad daylight – not cover of darkness as planned – included key industrial sites in Tokyo, Yokohama, Kobe and Nagoya. But then instead of fleeing on across to China in daylight, crews were forced to navigate their ally's 8,000 foot mountains at night.

The only plane that came down on its tricycle wheels landed in Russian; America's ally detained the crew for more than a year. All other planes were lost, crew members scattered.

On April 20, the day following the raid, the world's news organ verified the secret mission's success. Only then did personnel at Columbia Army Air Base (the name had changed April 2) learn of the brush they'd had with history.

Despite Japan's public denial the bombing did but little damage, international headlines roared that Doolittle's Raiders had done to Japan what the island nation's propaganda machine had said was impossible. Sixteen B-25s that had practiced pulling up before reaching the white line, launched from the pitching deck of an aircraft carrier more than 400 miles off the Japanese coast, had rained fury on the country that bombed Pearl Harbor.

From then on, pride by proxy pervaded Columbia Army Air Base. By transference, airmen assigned there and those yet to report to the site where it all began dared to speak their names in a sentence that also referenced Lt. Col. James Harold Doolittle. The legendary aviator's huge shadow had been cast across the growing airbase that took on the persona of the Doolittle Raiders.

Lt. Jimmy Doolittle added to the tips of bombs headed for Tokyo a handful of Japanese friendship medals, given to the U.S. by that country only months before the attack on Pearl Harbor.
Courtesy Martin Crouch

Months later, some of Doolittle's crew members still were still unaccounted for. Those who made it through the Chinese underground and were repatriated began the arduous process of putting the pieces into reports. On Friday, June 19, Doolittle was back on Columbia Army Air Base to whip up morale by discussing plans to speed up the operational training unit with the outfit's officials.

CHAPTER NINE

Photo by Bill Hamson

Sure, we want to go home. We want this war over with. The quickest way to get it over with is to go get the bastards who started it. The quicker they are whipped, the quicker we can go home. The shortest way home is through Berlin and Tokyo. And when we get to Berlin, I am personally going to shoot that paper hanging son-of-a-bitch Hitler. Just like I'd shoot a snake!

General George S. Patton
(addressing his troops
before Operation Overlord)
5th June 1944

CHAPTER NINE

1943

Developments on base continued into 1943; however, rapid expansion that had characterized previous months had leveled off. Well established units and up-and-running facilities were readily available to deal with new problems as they arose.

At the dawn of the new year, the base was accommodating: the Base Headquarters Squadron – which included Finance, Weather Station, Ordnance Detachment, Band – and other entities. A detachment of the Signal Service Corps was on base along with a detachment of the 903 Quartermaster Company, the 339th Aviation Squadron; both medical and veterinary detachments, the 309th Bombardment Group, which was a replacement training unit; the 65th Observation Group, also part of the replacement training unit, and a Chemical Service Detachment of the Air Service Command.

A new band director quickly assumed leadership of the base band late in January 1943; Marion Sell began expanding the band's functions. To base parades and official functions as well as entertainment were added appearances on other bases, and baseball games in town at Dreyfuss Park. When bond drives and rallies as well as military recruiting events were held, the band often performed.

As the popularity of the band grew, so did demands for its presence. A second dance band spun off the earlier success of the "Jive Bombers." When added to the regular military band, the "Naturals" brought to three the number of bands that could perform on or off base.

Also early that year, the base operated a number of schools such as the Celestial Navigation School, Clerks-Administrative School, Typing School, and schools for chemical gas officers and non-commissioned officers.

By February an altitude training unit, complete with a low-pressure chamber, also had been activated to augment lectures and movies presented to prepare airmen for changes that would affect them at high altitudes. The pressure chamber resembled a huge steel cylinder turned on its side. Its interior could accommodate ten men equipped with oxygen masks. The experience replicated an aerial climb to altitudes of 12,000 to 38,000 feet, common in runs made in medium bombers, with changes occurring just as they would on a flight.

That aspect of training also included orientations to the uses of emergency kits that contained self-inflating rafts, rations, fishing tackle, axe, knife, first aid kit, and other survival items.

With February came a team of warrant officers to take over the work of the 922 Quartermaster Boat Company site of the bombing range at Lake Murray.

Seven celestial navigation towers were operational by April 1943. The silo-like structures with octagonal sides accommodated an entire crew in a given training session: pilot, navigator, radio operator, and bombardier.

After intense days of training, personnel had steam to blow off but not enough recreational facilities in which to do so. It was softball season, and the only place to pitch and catch was a contractor's dump site. By clearing the area, some materials for a wooden grandstand were salvaged, a sand-clay infield was built and turf put down for an outfield. The improvement was so popular five additional diamonds were built for softball in other areas of the base complex.

Photograph by Bill Hamson

Before the base commander's spring fever subsided, he had designated for recreation three lakes that were part of the original tracts obtained from local landowners for the development of the base. The banks and fringes were cleared of unwanted vegetation, which also improved the spillway structure and the dam function; then the ponds were stocked with fish.

The pond outside the home in which Dr. I. B. Durham had resided became the officer's lake; the home was the officers' club. The lake adjacent to the home of Durham's brother, Dr. V. G. Durham, a dentist, was to be used for enlisted men's swimming. Sharp's Pond was for colored enlisted men.

Photograph by Bill Hamson

Opportunities for swimming were just one part of a comprehensive recreation plan aimed at affording personnel to change gears, build camaraderie, and enhance fitness for which individualized plans were developed and followed. Consistent reminders emphasized there also were opportunities for: basketball, with teams as well as an Inter-squadron League; boxing; and volleyball. Skeet shooting was simultaneously recreational and served equally well as training; airmen were encouraged to build their skills in their limited off-duty hours. By June 1943 a mandatory quarterly physical fitness test had been implemented.

June also marked the activation of the 910th WAAC Post Headquarters Company. Male personnel displayed their approval of having WACs in their midst after fifty-five enlisted women were sworn into the Army of the United States 6 August 1943. As they marched back to their place in line, the base band saluted them musically with the Army Air Corps Song.

Late in August the Base Engineer was called upon to construct temporary prisoner of war camps at four sites selected in South Carolina. When the prisoners arrived three days earlier than expected, the camps had to be completed in three days. Flood lighting and a sturdy fence were among the immediate construction needs; temporary kitchen and pit latrine considerations had been made prior to the prisoners' arrival.

Courtesy South Caroliniana Library

The Base Library moved to more suitable quarters during summer 1943; in September new bowling alleys opened, and recreation went high-tech on Labor Day when a track meet was started by remote control.

Later in September a special cooking school was set up for teaching cooks, including many from units stationed at nearby sub-bases, how to prepare meals from dehydrated foods.

Before the end of 1943, additional recreational facilities had been added. Expanding upon the function of several gymnasiums and the softball diamonds already in use were football fields, tennis courts, a field for track athletics (this in addition to the running track used for physical training), areas for ping pong and horseshoe pitching.

Photograph by Bill Hamson

By late year a Convalescent Training Program mandated by the Army Air Forces had proven successful. The premise of the program was to turn wasted days of hospitalization into training time so that subjects would be able to return to duty as soon as possible in as ready condition as possible. Calisthenics were an integral part of the program, but all patients would not have been able to participate, so there were lectures and films on topics ranging from First Aid to Tropical Diseases, Weather Theory, Military Intelligence, Bomb Reconnaissance and other subjects.

Before administrators closed out their year-end reports, the following units were operating under the auspices of CAAB: Walterboro Army Air Field – sub-base; Congaree Army Air Field – sub-base; Barnwell Army

Airfield – auxiliary field; Dublin Army Airport, auxiliary field, John's Island Airport – auxiliary field; North Army Airport – auxiliary field; and Ocean Drive Flight Strip, Wampee, SC – auxiliary field.

By October 12, 1943, when Col. Guy L. McNeill took command of the base, the early reputation of Lexington County Airport as a sandy lot dotted with scruffy pines and scrub oaks had been replaced. Now Columbia Army Air Base prided itself as a streamlined field whose theater-of-operations buildings, although designed for economy and constructed with great speed, were executed for efficiency.

As 1943 wound down, three WACs received overseas orders to report early in 1944 to receive training for their new assignments.

Photograph by Bill Hamson

CHAPTER TEN

Courtesy Dave and Marty Sennema Collection

Courage is fear holding on a minute longer.

        General George Patton

CHAPTER TEN

1944

The toll war was taking on personnel was reflected early in 1944 by the creation of the Replacement Depot to create a pool of airmen – officers and enlisted – to fill crew positions where casualties or changes in orders left openings. The operation's naturally-rapid personnel turnover brought to the base thousands of men in short order. Because many of the men had seen action in various combat theaters throughout the world, they brought with them information gleaned from their experiences and therefore became valuable in training arenas, both in classrooms and in the air.

Early in 1944 an extensive educational program, for both officers and enlisted personnel, included courses in: chemical warfare, camouflage, malarial control, field sanitation, personal hygiene, and map reading. All personnel received a course in safeguarding military information. Special schools instructed specialized classes in booby traps and bomb reconnaissance, and military law (officers only). In March that year, the Altitude Training School began an experimental class in Night Vision Training.

The Jam Handy Trainer, also begun early in 1944, used motion pictures to approximate for aerial gunners combat conditions. As film unreeled a trainee saw enemy aircraft of every class coming in his direction. A beam of light replaced ammunition; an infra-red scoring device scored the test for the duration of the two-hour class as members of combat crews took turns sighting and firing all guns a B-25 would carry.

Speaking of film, on 9 and 10 February, 1943, base personnel had the opportunity to view Metro-Goldwyn-Mayer's production, "A Guy Named Joe", part of which had been filmed at CAAB. A stash of two hundred free tickets was given, first dibs to those who had been on base during the filming and perhaps had even been involved. The movie house had to add an extra screening of the show to satisfy demands to see it. Proceeds from tickets sales made by those who did not qualify for a free one went to the Army Emergency Relief.

Late that month, former heavyweight champion Max Baer, now Staff Sergeant Baer, was featured in a boxing exhibition. The base often had celebrities from the world of entertainment or sports drop by, and those visits always pumped up morale, at least temporarily. Anyone with ties to the world outside the base had the potential for affecting morale positively. Even if the personality was not flesh and blood, the potential existed. For instance, cartoonist Sergeant Stan Drake, creator of cartoon character Penny Peex, was assigned to CAAB's Plane and Training Section of the Replacement Depot. Before he entered the military, Drake had a Hollywood movie contract. Now that he was in Columbia, his cartoon strip ran in the base's Winged Spirit newspaper.

To teach GIs the importance of camouflage in an entertaining way, a puppet show entitled "The Adventures of Snafu" was shown, courtesy of the Camouflage School on base.

Photo by Ed Benson

Late in May the Base Recreational Hall became the staging area for the first of a four-performance musical review its producers called "The Blue and Goldbrick Follies." By then there was, in addition to the band and several dance and specialty bands, a CAAB orchestra, conducted by Joe Garafola. The orchestra opened the follies with an overture. One number, "A Pretty Girl is Like a Melody" featured a male soloist and show girls. When "Poinciana" was played, a dance exhibition accompanied it. America was fascinated with the cultures of its South American neighbors, and that song epitomized the allure. In short order the three other performances were given, all at locations in Columbia.

Entertainment continued during the year with a number of concerts under the direction of Chief Warrant Officer Marian Sell, band leader. With a desire to strike a pleasing chord with everyone in the audiences, Sell incorporated all types of music – from Tin Pan Alley to Broadway, classics to novelty tunes.

As an example the program for a 30 March 1944 concert began with an overture, "Morning, Moon and Night in Vienna", by von Supps; "Pan Americana", a Latin-American number composed by Victor Herbert; a medley from "Oklahoma", an intermezzo, "In a Monastery Garden" by Ketelby, and a special arrangement of "When Uba Plays a Rumba on his Tuba".

Sell also led the band in his original march, "Spirit of Freedom".

The base's physical plant was ostensibly complete by 1944; however, the Base Engineer still was called up for occasional construction – such as a prisoner of war

Mary Merchant (Watson) worked at Citizens and Southern National Bank's on-base location. Courtesy Watson Collection

side camp in Barnwell, remodeling of the Post Exchange, and the remodeling of a building to house the base branch of Citizens and Southern Bank of South Carolina.

By 1944, the fairer sex had proven itself both ornamental and utilitarian on Columbia Army Air Base. Long before the arrival of the Women's Army Air Corps 14 June 1943, women had rolled their sleeves up alongside men working in civilian roles. In fact, one of the earliest official reports noted that women were used for all jobs they could handle effectively.

A WAC detachment activated as 810th WAAC Post Headquarters Company and was welcomed under Company Commander, Lt. Lelia Fay. Within a week more females had reported to base, justifying the opening of a mess hall expressly for them where previously females had been served in the hospital mess.

Two events important to the WACs occurred on the same day – July 15 – when the Beauty Shop opened and the first WAC wedding was solemnized on base.

To this point most of the work assigned WAACs had been in the hospital, but as their numbers grew, they were tasked with administrative duties. Others worked in the link training area as well as celestial navigation, along with base operations and the photo laboratory.

By the beginning of 1944, WACs had been integrated into jobs in the Base Operations Office where all air traffic was directed and controlled; in the Signal Office where they performed as teletype and telephone operators and messengers; at the Base Film Library where training films were archived and pulled for use; at the photostat machine and in the dark room. WACs were assigned to the Base Post Office, as Chaplain's assistant and organ accompanist, and in the Link Trainer area.

WACs helped staff recruiting booths at events around town and were highly visible at the 1943 South Carolina State Fair. Later that fall WACs were guests of Town Theater for a performance of the WAC play, "Show Me First."

Three (Women Air Force Service Pilots) WASPs were Thanksgiving guests on base in 1943, staying over in the WACs' barracks. One WASP, Susan Clarke, died in a crash as the plane she was piloting approached CAAB.

With the assistance of Gray Ladies, working alongside military base personnel, the Army Air Forces Convalescent Training Program was launched

Willodean Rion (Lumpkin).
Courtesy Lumpkin Collection

and made rapid progress in getting individuals back to their jobs as soon as possible.

With the establishment of a Home Hospitality Committee, hospital recre-

Courtesy Frances Addy Price

ational programming was enhanced by the screening of movies, along with entertainment featuring amateur talent or the playing of recorded music.

By mid-1944 WACs were being assigned to a wider range of jobs on base, from motor transport to operations – even aviation mechanics, especially if they came into the military already having those skills. Two were assigned to CAAB sub-bases.

Young ladies came to base for parties and Tuesday night dances, lifting the spirits of the airmen serving far from home. Trucks collected them from outlying neighborhoods and brought them onto base and got them safely home again to their families. The fairer sex invited airmen home for Sunday dinners and to attend area churches with them.

And it was not unusual for romance to blossom from these friendships. Photographers Ed Benson and Bill Hamson each met their brides while stationed at CAAB. "Tik" Tokaz married a University of South Carolina co-ed from Saluda whom he met while at CAAB.

Helen Townsend met and became the bride of OSS Officer Dan Peterson, and Dean Davenport, who became a Doolittle Raider and returned later as an instructor, met and married Mary Lowry, a local girl.

Photo by Bill Hamson

Columbia native Helen (Townsend) Peterson became the bride of OSS Officer Dan Peterson.
Courtesy the Peterson Collection.

CHAPTER ELEVEN

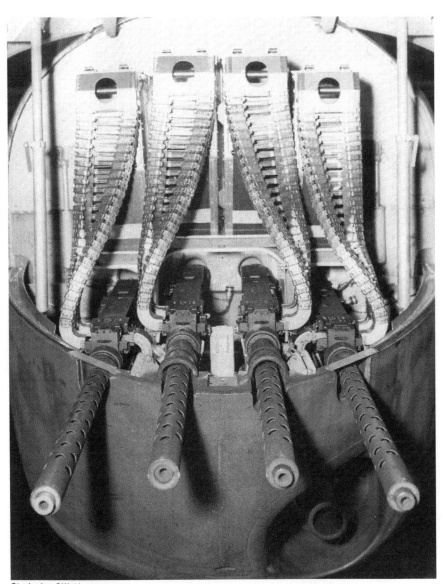

Photo by Bill Hamson

There is no substitute for victory.

                              General Douglas MacArthur

CHAPTER ELEVEN
1945

Personnel on base as the year 1944 gave way to 1945 were non-plused by rumors Columbia Army Air Base would be phasing out the B-25, around which their efforts had centered since the earliest days, in favor of the sleeker A-26.

Part of their reluctance to shift allegiance from one plane to another stemmed from their loyalty to the aircraft they felt personified CAAB – after all, it was the plane on which the Doolittle Raiders flew the Tokyo Raid. But they realized the needs of the war were changing, that the Allies needed attack planes, so they swallowed their objections and got busy PDQ learning how to operate, fly, and repair the A-26s that began arriving early in January. By the end of the month, fifteen A-26s were on the line. The men looked the other way as 26 B-25s were transferred out.

Another aspect of personnel's disinclination toward the change of planes the base would now use in training was that it also changed the base's status. Their apprehensions were warranted when, on 1 February 1945, the base left the Third Army and became the 329th Air Force Base Unit while the base became the 129th Army Air Base (Combat Crew Training Station – Low).

Servicemen convalescing on 21 January 1945 were treated to a medicinal concert by famed master musician Jose Iturbi who entertained personnel at the Red Cross Recreation Hall in the base hospital with a program that ran the gamut from classical and Gershwin to pop and boogie woogie. When he appeared at CAAB, Iturbi had played the part of himself two years earlier in the 1943 musical, "Thousands Cheer," as well as in the 1945 film, "Anchors Aweigh," in which he shared billing with Gene Kelly and Frank Sinatra.

Morale and therapeutic value of keeping the hobby shop open extended the hours to 11 p.m. to accommodate service personnel who were clocking long hours to keep planes in the air and crews ready to ship out. In this shop personnel enjoyed carving, throwing pots, woodwork of various kinds, leather craft and – new and novel – creating gift items from Plexiglas.

Someone on base came up with a design to create tiny pianos of the acrylic plastic that had been patented in 1933 by Otto Rohm. Personnel on base were familiar with the material as it appeared on B-25s in the nose cone. The miniature pianos made in the hobby shop were used as jewelry or cigarette cases, or to hold mementoes, so they became coveted gift items.

Morale suffered when, on 15 April 1945, news broke that President Franklin Delano Roosevelt had died – one state away, in Georgia. Troops assembled on the parade grounds to pay respects to the Commander in Chief who had led them through the war, to that date.

Later that month, just ten days before the departure of the 319th Bombardment Group was scheduled for the commencement of a new mission, generals and other high ranking officers of the First Air Force and the 56th Bombardier Training Wing visited both CAAB and the bombing range in Hartsville to review demonstrations of bombing capabilities attendant to the A-26. Simulating a recent tactical situation witnessed in the China-Burma-India Theater, the A-26s demonstrated low-level bombing and strafing.

The biggest day of 1945 was D-Day – June 6! Although personnel whooped it up, choosing to believe war's end was in sight, they knew better than to falter at such an important stage in the bid for freedom.

Tracking the pace of the war had heightened the sense of geography for every airman on base. Most – whether enlisted or recruited – had little worldly experience beyond their homes. They had arrived at CAAB from two or three previous training bases, and oftentimes, had not gotten to know the previous cities to which those training assignments took them. Now they were sharing barracks and cockpits with airmen from all over the country. Like all bases, CAAB was a melting pot.

It was stunning for base personnel who had not yet experienced combat to have "cultural exchanges" right there on base. While it was well known that German POWs were sequestered at the edge of the base, fraternization was not permitted. Still more stunning was the rare glimpses of Chinese pilots, on base for training, just as the American personnel was. The Chinese were watched with great scrutiny – and fascination – but not in the same way the Germans were monitored.

CHAPTER TWELVE

Training and safety went hand in glove with morale.
Photo by Bill Hamson

God of our fathers, who by land and sea has ever lead us to victory, please continue your inspiring guidance in this the greatest of all conflicts. Strengthen my soul so that the weakening instinct of self-preservation, which besets all of us in battle, shall not blind me to my duty, to my own manhood, to the glory of my calling, and to my responsibility to my fellow soldiers. Grant to our armed forces that disciplined valor and mutual confidence which insures success in war. Let me not mourn for the men who have died fighting, but rather let me be glad that such heroes have lived. If it be my lot to die, let me do so with courage and honor in a manner which will bring the greatest harm to the enemy, and please, oh Lord, protect and guide those I shall leave behind. Give us the victory, Lord.

General George Patton

CHAPTER TWELVE

Training and safety=morale

For an installation pushed into utilization hastily, the Lexington County Airport surfaced with surprising speed and efficiency. Admittedly, speed and safety can be polar opposites. But from the time the War department determined the purpose of the installation was to serve as a medium bomber training base, safety for personnel, as well as families whose properties abutted the complex, was a paramount priority. Thus, the decision that the base would be the take off and landing strip for B-25s set off many other decisions, especially with regard to safety.

Training and safety were not Either/Or choices on this base. Any lines of demarcation that indicated where training left off and safety picked up, and how training and safety factored into overall morale on base often were blurred.

Essential were instructions in combat survival, ranging from aspects of chemical warfare to high altitude flying, as well as escape and rescue tactics. Simulations often were part of the training, on ground and in the air. Every training mission was undertaken with the "real thing" at the center of the experience. Every close call that was pulled out successfully was celebrated. Every mishap brought back the blues, but there was no place for them to be exhibited. On the uniform blouses of trainees – even officers – there was no place on sleeves for wearing emotions. Because war didn't pause for grief or reflection, neither could combat crews readying to fight in it. Life on base went on.

Crewmen's gas masks could be their life preservers.

Gas mask training chamber.
Photo by Bill Hamson

Airmen who arrived at this base already had completed not only basic training but one or two more levels of flight training – and they were young, many coming off America's farms willing and able to transfer their experience with keeping tractors running to keeping airplane engines running. Manual labor had strengthened musculature and healthy food put away at family tables had strengthened their "constitutions". So, they were in the best shape they were ever likely to be. Officers on base wanted to keep it that way.

To assure the men got the physical training they needed, PT officers held weekly meetings with unit supervisors. Calisthenics helped keep personnel limber and nimble. Through woods that, only a couple of years earlier had been farmland, narrow trails had been cut; personnel ran these trails as part of their comprehensive physical training.

This is where the blurred lines come in: sports enhanced physical conditioning, but it was also a way for airmen to blow off steam at the end of stressful days of aerial training. It also pitted individuals against – and for – each other, building camaraderie and esprit de corps. In addition to regular PT, softball and baseball teams were organized and a schedule of games began with teams located near the base.

Volleyball offered airmen who had been confined in tight quarters all day a chance to stretch.
Photo by Bill Hamson

Soon an inter-squadron basketball league was formed; boxing was organized and encouraged via matches and shows that stimulated interest in the program. Additionally, ping pong and bowling were available, and volleyball courts were set up. Before the base concluded operations, there were tennis courts. Skeet shooting was strongly encouraged as a form of competition with self as well as target practice, especially for gunners.

Dr. Durham's home became Officer's Club; his pond a place for officers to swim.
Photo by Bill Hamson

Weather permitting, personnel enjoyed swimming on several ponds on or near base. Officers were allowed to swim in the pond adjacent to the

Officers' Club which had, before the war, been the home of Dr. Durham. Enlisted men swam in another pond, and there was a third for colored service personnel.

"Leg up" for morale

Pin-up girls boost morale.
Photo by Bill Hamson

Mailroom.
Photo by Bill Hamson

In a setting where security and secrecy were essential, some of the information enlisted personnel wanted most had to be kept under wraps; only top ranking officers with high-level clearances were privy to classified information. Censors had read every love letter penned to every airman. So, as an attempt to balance the areas in which information could not flow freely, the base commander rubber stamped his approval for the publishing of an on-base newsletter.

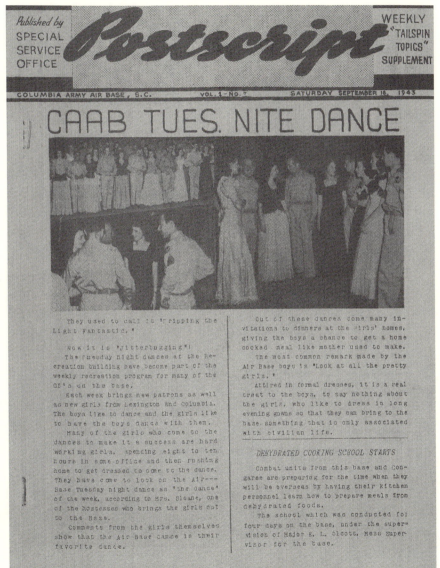

Courtesy Frances Addy Price

The need for communication and self-expression was relieved on 1 July 1942 with the issue of the first on-base newspaper, Tailspin Topics. At first, the publication was a few mimeographed sheets of news, cartoons and comments on affairs, both on and around the base, but over coming months it grew in importance as an anticipated release of information. Other on-base publications were Winged Spirit and the Postscript.

Even the addition of a public address system in high traffic areas was a form of morale improvement because it enabled personnel to get information quickly, directly, from a voice they recognized as having the appropriate authority to be transmitting information.

Mail call had the potential for being either a morale boost or bust. If a highly anticipated letter was not in the appropriate slot, it could bring on the blues.

An aural diversion from the thrum of airplane engines was promised on 14 July 1942 when the first on-base band was organized. After a month of practice, squeezed into unscheduled moments following long days of aerial training, the band members parked a crash truck outside the Finance Building, assembled its instruments in the flatbed, and gave its first performance

The band and its music might as well have been the Pied Piper because when there was music, there were girls, the magic elixir for the boosting of GI morales. Dances became regular Tuesday night event, something to look forward to, something to punch up the weekdays. With coordination by the USO, light-on-their-feet females from the surrounding neighborhoods and communities were collected and brought to base. Their mode of transport? A heavy 2x2 truck in whose bed rough wooden benches had been installed so the ladies could sit more properly; otherwise, their evening gowns would get wrinkled before they arrived at the dances.

From the original band, whose official duties involved performing in parades and at reviews, and entertaining dignitaries – both military and civilian – who came onto base, multiple other musical ensembles spun off. In time there were several dance bands, and an ensemble that performed more classical numbers, often in Columbia venues. Not only because they were the first spin-off but also because of their reputation for cranking out lively, dancable numbers, the Jive Bombers were a favorite.

Front row: Pfc. Lee D'Imperio, Sgt. James Hill, Sgt. Stanley La Vignes, Cpl.. Louis Herandiz, Sg.t Charles Pivovarsky, Sgt. Milford Allen, Pfc. Joseph Garofalo. Second row: Cpl Alton Schoadl, Cpl. John Murphy, Sgt. Edgar Calvert, Sgt. Rudyard Blume, Sgt. Kenneth Martens. M/Sgt Patrick Brogan.Piano- Pft. Monroe Sabal.
Photo courtesy Frances Addy Price.

Aside from the Tuesday night dances, there were parties thrown around the base at other times when the rigorous training schedule permitted. No excuse was too flimsy; however, the last night before crews were shipping out was a reason warranting a party, without need for any other justification.

All was not gloom on Columbia Army Air Base during WWII.
Photo by Bill Hamson

Airmen return from combat with valuable lessons to share

One of the biggest boosts to morale came from airmen who winged their way to base directly following combat duty. Crew members back from European, North African or Pacific tours had much to teach – about B-25s and their performance, about the enemy, about survival. Some of these airmen had been reassigned as instructors on base; some were awaiting orders or replacements for the crews. Some were convalescing. Their instruction was both formal and informal; it was given in ground school and around a table in the smoke-filled officers' club. It was yelled over the loud and steady thrum of Mitchell bomber engines. Trainees responded to it because it was current and real. It was the voice of experience. And it was speaking to them.

Lt. Colonel Jimmy Doolittle (1896-1993)

The returning airman who boosted morale more than any other during the short service life of the airbase was Jimmy Doolittle. He had been Lt. Colonel on his first visit to base and Brigadier General Doolittle when he returned June 19, 1942, less than two months after the raid on which he was followed off the pitching deck of the aircraft carrier USS Hornet by 15 other crews, all of whom had volunteered for the mission shortly after arriving on the base.

The War department had the newly-promoted general on a morale tour soon after he and all the crews he could reassemble were spirited out of China in a C-47 following the April 18, 1942, aerial attack on industrial targets in and near Tokyo, Japan. His time back on the base where it had all started was brief, but powerful.

Astronaut Deke Slayton (1924-1993)

Aside from Doolittle, the returning instructor airman who ultimately had the highest visibility would only have been considered one of the rank and file in the '40s. His high visibility came later. During both his times at Columbia Army Air Base, he was still known as Don (Donald) Slayton, but by the end of the following decade his astronaut buddies had nicknamed him Deke. Don Slayton had two assignments at Columbia Army Air Base: one near the beginning of his flying career and another soon after he had experienced first combat.

Slayton entered the Air Force as an aviation cadet and received his wings in April 1943 after completing flight training at Vernon and Waco, Texas. Following his combat crew training at CAAB, he was given clearance as a B-25 pilot with the 340th Bombardment Group. He flew 56 combat missions in Europe. He returned to the United States in mid-1944 as a B-25 instructor pilot back at CAAB, and later served with a unit responsible for checking pilot proficiency in the A-26.

In April 1945, he was sent to Okinawa with the 319th Bombardment Group and flew seven combat missions over Japan. He served as a B-25 instructor for one year following the end of the war and subsequently left the Air Force to enter the University of Minnesota. He became an aeronautical engineer after graduation and worked for two years with the Boeing Aircraft Corporation at Seattle, Washington, before being recalled to active duty in 1951 with the Minnesota Air National Guard.

Upon reporting for duty, he was assigned as maintenance flight test officer of an F-51 squadron located in Minneapolis, Minnesota, followed by 18-months as a technical inspector at Headquarters Twelfth Air Force, and a similar tour as fighter pilot and maintenance office with the 36th Fighter Day Wing at Bitburg, Germany.

Returning to the United States in June 1955, he attended the USAF Test Pilot School at Edwards Air Force Base, California. He was a test pilot there from January 1956 until April 1959 and participated in the testing of fighter aircraft built for the United States Air Force and some foreign countries.

Slayton was named as one of the seven Mercury astronauts in April 1959. He was originally scheduled to pilot the Mercury-Atlas 7 mission in 1959, but was relieved of this assignment due to a heart condition discovered during a physical.

He logged more than 6,600 hours flying time, including 5,100 hours in jet aircraft.

When CAAB-trained airmen, back from combat and assigned state-side led instructions on the base, their lessons took on believable importance for the trainees. This practice was one of CAAB's keys to success. That they returned was a morale booster in itself. And the context they added helped the lessons hit home with the trainees. By offering training and instruction in certain phases of combat preparation, these seasoned airmen could pass along first-hand information of the enemy's tactics, often gained at high altitudes, sometimes at high costs, and always through personal experience.

Col. Dean Davenport (1918-2000)

The return of Captain Dean Davenport, here initially with the 17th Bomb Group, the airmen pool from which volunteers were chosen for Doolittle's secret mission, was recalled by photographer William Hamson. Davenport became his commanding officer.

"He was a favorite with the men not only because of his role in the Doolittle Raid, but for his fair and common sense approach to leadership. There had been problems in the barracks with items disappearing. Davenport called the squadron together, let it be known he was aware of the problem, and ended the meeting with the warning: 'When you find him, don't bring him to me.' We took that to mean we could solve the problem on our own, but with Davenport's position on the matter noted, the problem ended." Davenport's service at CAAB was both a boost to base morale and invaluable training background.

Second Lieutenant Davenport was co-pilot of Ruptured Duck, the seventh plane off the Hornet deck, following the leader – Lt. Col. Jimmy Doolittle – for the daring raid over Tokyo. Davenport was flying right seat next to First Lieutenant Ted Lawson. After the Ruptured Duck's crew hit its target, a Japanese steel plant, it crashed into the East China Sea, a quarter mile from a beach on which the pilot was attempting to reach for a safe landing.

Upon impact, Lawson and Davenport were catapulted through the plane's windshield; Lawson sustained facial injuries and a gash in his leg that ultimately required amputation. Davenport fractured a leg and suffered a concussion. The other airmen got out, swam to the beach, and the crew was picked up by Chinese guerrillas who conveyed them by crude local means - Chinese-manned chairs, rickshaws and trucks – to a pick up site from which they were flown out of China.

The ordeal of the Ruptured Duck's crew was recounted in 1943 by the newly-promoted Captain Lawson in "Thirty Seconds Over Tokyo", written while he was convalescing from the amputation of his left leg. The book described the moment when the battered lieutenants found each other on the Chinese beach: "Speaking, and the sight of each other, seemed to bring us further along toward complete consciousness and both of us began to moan, standing there next to each other in the black rain."

Lieutenant Davenport was a technical adviser for the 1944 movie "Thirty Seconds Over Tokyo," in which he was portrayed by Tim Murdock. For the filming of the movie, Davenport flew a B-25 bomber off a pier in Santa Monica, California, in a scene depicting the departure from the Hornet. The Army Air Forces also allowed him to fly in the wartime movie "A Guy Named Joe", an aviation fantasy, some of which – ironically – was shot on Columbia Army Air Base.

Later in the war, Davenport served in Alaska, flying P-40, P-38 and P-51 aircraft. Davenport remained in the service after World War II and returned to combat in the Korean War, flying 86 missions as a fighter pilot. He was commanding officer of several fighter units, including the Air Defense Command's 325th Fighter Wing, flying F-106 interceptors.

He retired as a colonel in 1967. In addition to the Distinguished Flying Cross, he was awarded the Silver Star, Legion of Merit, Air Medal and the Air Force Commendation Medal with one oak leaf cluster. For his part in the Tokyo raid, he was awarded the Chinese Army/Navy/Air Corps medal, Class A, 1st Grade.

One of Hamson's favorite photographs is of Davenport on his way to the mezzanine of the Columbia Hotel for an officers' dance.

Capt. Dean Davenport and Mary Lowry.
Photo by Bill Hamson.

Adolph "Tik" Tokaz (1913-2001)

"Tik" Tokaz began training the first permanently stationed B-25 crews at Columbia Army Air Base in August 1942, having arrived from Dale Mabry Field, Florida, where he volunteered for combat duty. The 3rd Air Force headquarters in Tampa assigned him to the 309th Bomb Group at Columbia Army Air Base.

Tokaz arrived in Columbia and received orders on 20 August, 1942 to stand up the 340th Bomb Group from the commanding officer Colonel Nedwed of the 309th Bomb Group. Tokaz received orders later to activate the 340th Bomb Group on 3 September 1943 in a tiny office on CAAB and was its first commanding officer. Lt Colonel Tokaz was replaced later that month by Colonel William Mills, commanding officer of the historic 17th Bomb Group from which the Doolittle Raider volunteers were drawn in Columbia. Tokaz became Mills' executive officer, and later his operations officer. When Mills was killed in action in North Africa 6 May 1943, Tokaz again became commanding officer of the 340th Bomb Group.

During the North African Campaign, Tokaz's bomb group flew against Field Marshall Rommel's Axis forces. The 340th Bomb Group was heavily involved in the bombing of enemy troops, fortifications, and supply lines throughout the Mediterranean theatre of operations. When the first Italian pilots defected from the Italian Air Force, they surrendered to Lt Colonel Tokaz at an allied airfield in Catania, Sicily, on 13 September 1943. This event was recorded by the Movietone News Service and narrated by the famous correspondent Lowell Thomas. The footage was shown in movie theatres throughout America. Tokaz then transferred as American Liaison Officer (ALO) to the Tactical Bomber Force, Air Officer Commanding (AOC) Air Commodore Sinclair of

the RAF. When the 57th Bomb Wing was formed under the command of General Robert D. Knapp, Tokaz became the Operations Officer of the 57th Bomb Wing.

He returned to CAAB in June 1944, and served as Director of Operations and Training until the base's deactivation in November 1945. He moved from CAAB to Shaw Field as the Base Executive Officer where Chinese air crews were being trained in the B-25. He was transferred in the summer of 1947 to Yokota Air Force Base, Japan as executive officer of an A-26 bomb group that was part of the Allied Occupation Forces. He then was transferred to the Air Staff of General Douglas MacArthur's Headquarters in Tokyo. He returned to the CONUS in 1950 at Mitchel Field, New York as part of the 1st Air Force headquarters..

In 1952 Tokaz served as a member of a secret project in the Pacific at Kwajalein Island and piloted the C-47 transport aircraft from which the Air Force aerial photographer took the official photograph of the first hydrogen bomb explosion. That photograph was published in newspapers worldwide.

Tokaz later served as Deputy Commander for Personnel at Robins AFB, Georgia, and as the commanding officer, Air Reserve Center, New Orleans. He retired in 1961 as Deputy Chief of Staff for Personnel, Reserve Affairs at the Pentagon in Washington DC, and returned to Columbia in retirement. His wife, Frances Jones, was from Saluda, SC; they had met in Columbia where she was a student at the University of South Carolina and he was a captain assigned to Owens Field. They married in June 1940.

Morale was handled as a high priority on and around CAAB. Keeping personnel safe, via solid training and frequent testing, did much for keeping morale up throughout the complex. Even when convalescing in the base hospital, personnel members were engaged in programs to keep them involved in day to day operations so they could return to their posts as soon as possible, in duty-ready condition.

Photo by Bill Hamson

CHAPTER THIRTEEN

Photo by Bill Hamson

Military power wins battles, but spiritual power wins wars.

General George Catlett Marshall

CHAPTER THIRTEEN
Around Town

The buzz around town in 1940 was that a new airport was to be developed in Columbia – as a commercial facility, but to be undertaken with all specifications it would need should war – already raging in Europe – make it necessary for the government to take over.

Springdale, as it is known today, was the area from which property was absorbed for the airport development. Taken by eminent domain, the land was in Lexington County, thus the original name of the facility. The close-knit community that surrounded the base complex was not yet incorporated. Land owned and farmed by branches of the prolific Roof family was taken, or purchased under legal duress, for the original components of the base and, in 1943, for expansion.

The late Jimmy Roof created, from family records and his father Jobe's recollections, a rough plat map showing how family properties aligned, pre-WWII, with a network of dirt roads, intersecting with Platt Springs Road, and SC Hwy. 215 (now 302). Those family tracts had been divided only by friendly fences before representatives of the South Carolina Aeronautics Commission came calling. Owners Alton, Frank, John, Charlton, and Jobe Roof all lost their farms and homes to the development. Additionally, there was Kyzer, Sox, and Kinsler property taken; the home of Dr. Clayton Durham became the Officers' Club on base.

Neighbors on the periphery of the base still include in their family lore stories about having airmen – and German POWs – in their midst, and airplanes replacing cows in their vistas. Three generations after her great-grandfather lost his land to a new crop – B-25s – Anna Wilkerson wrote a paper for a school assignment, using her grandfather Jimmy Roof as her primary resource.

"Two of the worst crashes took place within a mile of the airbase. One took place right in front of where Springdale Elementary School is now. A pilot was flying and his plane caught on fire. He tried to bail, but his parachute did not open. His plane crashed into a tree that is now bent as a result. Another plane carried seven men. Their plane hit at the corner, where Ermine Road is now. A man ran to save them. He was able to save three; they had to watch as the others, pinned in, burned to death. It was said to be a truly horrific experience."

Residents who were very young at the time recall being frightened at the presence of German POWs in the neighborhood. Their camp was situated where Airport High School is located today.

As part of the land takeover agreement, the government offered employment to farmers who lost their livelihoods to the property takeover. Jobe Roof was put in charge of maintenance in the mess hall for the prisoners. In young Anna Wilkerson's report is a photograph of Jobe Roof standing behind a truck; in the back were members of his maintenance crew.

It was not until 2 April 1942 that a letter received from the War department officially changed the name to Columbia Army Air Base. Development of the base brought revenues into both Lexington and Columbia, and utilized the resources of both.

COLUMBIA ARMY AIR BASE

Citizens throughout the midlands were generous with their time, talent and the limited other resources available during tough war times.

Buildings could not be erected fast enough to keep pace with the arrival of airmen for their combat training, and the supplies and equipment they would need, so the War department leased out some buildings in downtown Columbia to absorb some of the quartermaster's storage needs.

COLUMBIA, SOUTH CAROLINA

The airport's affect on local real estate stretched far beyond its security gate.

One was an old wholesale grocery building which was converted into a commissary. A garage at the corner of Sumter and Blanding streets became a warehouse for clothing and equipment. And the base had used telephone lines supplied by Southern Bell Telephone and Telegraph Company in the early months of its operations. Eventually, as new buildings were ready for occupancy, enlisted men from the Signal Service Company arrived under Special Orders to set up communications systems on base, also occupied by the Base Post Office.

Personnel less likely to be shipped overseas on short notice were allowed to find accommodations in town – if they could. Some hotels had been converted to apartments; regular sleeping rooms were continually booked. The Lexington County Airport only taxed further the demands for temporary lodging; military personnel coming from and going to Fort Jackson already had accommodations maxed out.

So, many Columbians turned spare bedrooms into boarding rooms for military personnel assigned to the new facility. Their hospitality reached far beyond their homes and porches, well into the community, and even onto the base site.

Bill Hamson gets a bird's eye view of Columbia's Main Street.

While the base was inching its way toward becoming fully operational, facilities as well as personnel dedicated to recreation were understandably limited, so as often as schedules permitted, airmen partook of local hospitality. Downtown theatres gained khaki-clad audiences, restaurants filled requests to create menu items reminiscent of "home cooking", wherever home was.

Leave time was a precious commodity, but when service personnel did get time off, they came into town and explored what was, for many, a first exposure to a Southern venue, a Capital City, a town that had a vibrant Main Street.

When the first amateur show organized on base was ready for presentation in late summer of 1942, inclement weather forced planners to seek a dry stage, so the event was moved in town to the USO in downtown Columbia.

Photo by Bill Hamson

One of the most joyous occasions that brought together Columbians and military personnel was the 1942 Christmas party airmen threw for seventy-five orphans residing at Epworth Children's Home. The account of the party published in the post-holiday edition of Winged Spirit, the on-base newspaper, gave the details.

The children arrived in GI vehicles and assembled in the gym where they were entertained by the CAAB band. Christmas dinner was served in various mess halls, and in the afternoon children and airmen returned to the gym and the decorated Christmas tree. Beneath the tree were gifts for the children, many of which had been hand-made by airmen in the base craft shop. Before the children were transported back to Epworth, they had fun participating in games organized by base personnel.

The crash boat crew had only two boats to use in picking up crews from planes that went into Lake Murray during training bombing missions: one was a Chris-Craft; the other an old tug. Early in March 1943, Dr. Vandergrift of Columbia lent his boat to the effort.

Columbia's formal introduction to CAAB was made 27 September 1943 during "This is the Army" Parade, one highlight of an Army Emergency Relief Drive sponsored that month by the Civil Air Patrol. Following the parade down Main Street, there was a program at Owens Field. Joining personnel from CAAB were navy cadets and army personnel from Fort Jackson. A screening of the movie, "This is the Army", was shown as public incentive to participate in the initiative to step up recruiting. Also that fall, the base was represented in a recruiting booth set up at the South Carolina State Fair.

Newsboys from around town were brought to base for a fieldtrip, also in September 1943. More than a hundred newsboys went home that evening to regale their families with accounts of their sights and the sounds of B-25 bombers, their handshakes with pilots, airplane mechanics, and other personnel.

Photo by Ed Benson

Late in October WACs were guests of Town Theater for a performance of the WAC play, "Show Me First."

Another parade marched through downtown Columbia on Armistice Day 1943; as a finale, a formation of B-25 bombers flew overhead. The parade ended at the State House steps which became the staging area for a pageant-type show with musical highlights from the base band and quartet, along with a WAC trio, and speeches from both civilian and military spokesmen.

Note: Set aside, following WWI, Armistice Day has been a day of remembrance:The day of the Allies and Germany signing, in Compiegne, France, papers that officially ended the Great War. Pens were drawn and ready on the eleventh hour, eleventh day, eleventh month. That day now is celebrated annually as Veterans' Day.

Late in May 1944 the Base Recreational Hall became the staging area for the first of a four-performance musical review that its producers called "The Blue and Goldbrick Follies." The three other performances were given off base: at the USO in downtown Columbia, Fort Jackson and the Township Auditorium. Belk's Department Store provided dresses for one of the female trios, and the spotlights used were on loan from Carolina Theatre.

Dancing and singing acts, skits, stage settings and lighting effects gave the follies a sophisticated allure. The production promoted the Fifty War Bond Drive; admission was one war bond, with $1,500,000 in bonds selling over the four-performance run of the production.

To keep up a keen interest in enlisting – especially for the WAC units – CAAB was invited to put on a radio program in town, broadcast from the lobby of the Wade Hampton Hotel. Another radio program, this one airing nationally from the ballroom of the Columbia Hotel, featured a competition between a team from CAAB and Fort Jackson. The CAAB team was winner of the contest sponsored by the United States Rubber Corporation.

Columbian James C. Jackson took a $300 prize offered by the Committee for Civilian Employee Suggestions for three advancements in tools he designed that saved manpower in the aircraft repair shop. This was the largest award made to a civilian, but Jackson's real pride was in the fact that his designs were forwarded to Wright Field where they were distributed to all other air force repair shops.

The arrival of D-Day diminished in no way the dogged intensity or prevailing sense of purpose exhibited by the united front, not on CAAB, and not throughout Columbia. If anything, the need for efforts to keep morale

Christie Zimmerman broadcast local news for WIS Radio.

up were more important than ever – the goal was in sight!

But officials and private citizens were anticipating already that when the hard-fought-for freedom prevailed and the war ended, all the military personnel returning home would be looking for jobs. The last week in February 1945, an event sponsored by the Laurel Street USO, along with businessmen and professionals, was held at the Township Auditorium, billed as "New Horizons." Today it might be billed as a job fair.

Exhibits showcased prospects in new fields of endeavor for which GIs were likely to qualify in the coming post-war period: electronics, aeronautics, and construction. Attractions that drew the largest groups of visitors were motion picture and television demonstrations, along with an engineering display by Pratt and Whitney, Inc. Manufactured items of plastics or cotton material were also of great interest.

Slim was the attendance by the personnel for whom the event was targeted – they had noses to grindstones finalizing the war. But the effort demonstrated foresight, the elicited hope throughout the community that there would be jobs waiting when Johnny Came Marching Home.

Lake Murray and its surrounding communities, such as Chapin, would, in no way, have been considered In Town. The population living around the lake was meager at the time. Yet, the lake's importance to Columbia Army Air Base and the aviation successes made possible by bombing training missions over the vast waterway linked the two in history inextricably.

Built to produce hydroelectric power, the 50,000 acre impoundment of the Saluda River lying ten miles northwest of CAAB had been functioning since September 1930 when, at that time, it enjoyed the distinction of being the largest earthen dam constructed.

Research has not revealed whether proximity and access to such an ideal training venue affected the survey committee's early-1942 decision that CAAB would specialize in the training of B-25 crews and entire units. It is known that the U.S. War Department leased land around the lake, sparsely populated during most of the year, and uncrowded even during vacation months. Some of the islands protruding above the water's surface were of an ideal size for target practice. They were naturally isolated so that fire resulting from training accidents could be contained easily, and civilians were not close by. Islands used for target practice included Shull and Wessinger. Lunch Island was called by several other names including Goat Island. Eventually, the name Doolittle Island was added to the list of monikers.

The air base made an indelible impression on the South Carolina midlands, and the sights and sounds of aircraft overhead affected the career, or at least service, decisions of many young men. They, too, wanted to fly.

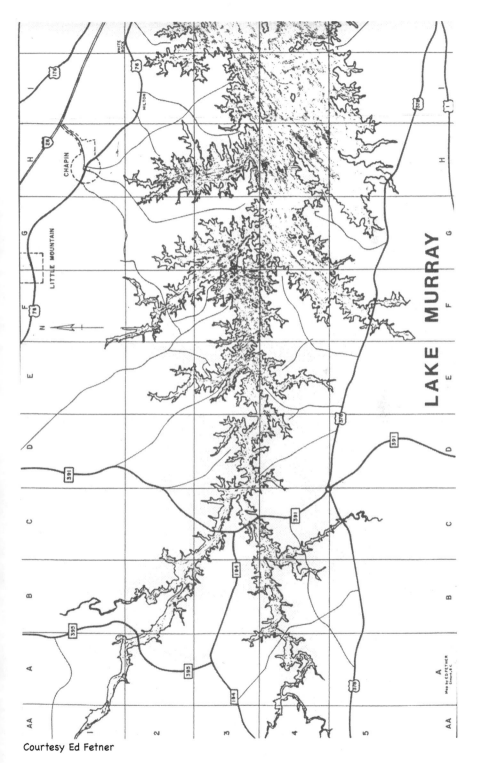
Courtesy Ed Fetner

CHAPTER FOURTEEN

Photo of Lt. Col. Jimmy Doolittle by Ed Benson.

I hate war as only a soldier who has lived it can, only as one who has seen its brutality, its futility, its stupidity.

> General Dwight D. Eisenhower

CHAPTER FOURTEEN

Eye-witness Accounts

These individuals have provided eye witness or legacy accounts attendant to time spent on or around Columbia Army Air Base

James Hare, an eye witness, was dazzled by the notion of flying even before news enveloped his close-knit neighborhood – an airport was to be constructed nearby. "Columbia was quite excited about all the possibilities that came with the announcements," said Lt. Col. James Hare, retired, a West Columbia resident again after completing a long and decorated military career in which he flew 100 missions.

For this impressionable young man, living in the proximity of an emerging airbase was a large part of his aviation inspiration. Watching as farmland was bulldozed into airstrips brought his youthful dreams within reach.

"My dad would take us over there to see how much progress had been made since the last time. By the time the base opened, I was already in service."

His family lived at 412 Spring Street in West Columbia in a home his mother built next to her own mother's home. "Once the base opened, my mother worked on flight suits at a sewing machine in the fabric shop on base. My sister was in training to become a junior mechanic and my youngest brother trained to be an aircraft mechanic. Another brother trained at Palmetto School of Aviation." Another brother opted for the Navy. "He was to be in naval aviation, but the war ended before he finished his training."

With two older brothers already in the military, it was hard for Hare to wait, so as soon as he was old enough, he went down to the Assembly Street recruiting office and signed up. He was going to fly an airplane. As an aviation cadet, he still had a wait before a flying school slot opened. In Ballinger, Texas, he was introduced to the single engine, PT-19. He advanced several rungs more on the training ladder in Texas before he ultimately was sent to Sarasota, Florida, for his check flight in a P-40.

Although Hare never was assigned to Columbia Army Air Base, or Lexington County Airport – the facility's first name, he did fly out of the base – to give his mother a flight.

"I was home on furlough and was able to borrow one of the planes so I could take her up. She was around planes all the time, but she'd never flown. She loved it! She had always encouraged all us kids to be whatever we wanted to be. I loved to fly!"

His combat unit joined another unit in Sicily in April 1943 for what became known as the Cape Bon Massacre or the Palm Sunday Massacre, part of Operation Flax, a Western Allies operation executed to cut supply lines between Italy and Axis armies.

"I was a wing man first, then a flight leader and, ultimately, a squadron leader," recalled Hare, who signed on for a second tour of duty, rejoining his group in Italy. "I love the P-47. It's a very reliable plane," Hare said.

His unit had been on the east coast of Italy, but then moved to Naples on the west coast. "Then they moved us to Corsica; that would put us closer to German lines." From Grossetta, Italy, his entire outfit moved up the Poe Valley. "The Germans finally surrendered at Villafranca. From there we were supposed to go to the Far East. We got a couple of days from the Panama Canal when the second atomic bomb was dropped, of course, changing our course."

Hare remained in service after the war ended, was assigned to Shaw Field and flew missions again during the Korean War. He was promoted to the rank of Colonel in 1963; the following year he was assigned as Commandant of the Fighter Weapons School and was made Wing Deputy for Operations the following year. In late 1965 he was assigned to the Fighter Section 9th Air Force, Shaw AFB, SC. When he retired from military service in 1967, he had a second career in state government with the South Carolina Department of Vocational Rehabilitation in Columbia.

Ed Benson was in the first wave of airmen to receive orders for Lexington County Airport in the early months following the U.S. government takeover; which came just hours after the Japanese attacked Pearl Harbor. The airport had been nearly ready to open and begin operations as a commercial facility on December 7, 1941.

Part of the 17th Bombardment Group assigned to Pendleton Air Base in Oregon, just prior to the Columbia, South Carolina assignment, Benson

Ed Benson was part of the photographic detail for the 17th Bomb Squadron sent to Columbia Army Air Base from Pendleton, Oregon. Photographs from his collection are used throughout this book.
Photo courtesy Ed Benson

arrived early in February 1942. As part of his squadron's photographic detail, he captured some of the base's early history, including the February visit of Lt. Col. Jimmy Doolittle. One of his photographs from that historic event appears on the cover of this book.

Missing the wide open spaces of his native Idaho, he went walking down one of the roads near the base one afternoon. "I noticed a couple of people up on a roof, doing some work. It reminded me of the kind of chores I'd done on the ranch back home, so I asked them if they'd like some help. I crawled up the ladder and helped them, they invited me to stay for dinner, and I met the younger sister of the woman whose roof was getting repaired."

He married that Columbia girl, Betty Ray Sox, and they farmed together in Idaho – wheat, alfalfa, barley, oats, hay and some cattle – until she died a few years ago. Now residing in Montana with his daughter B.J. Hultz, Benson shoveled the season's first snow in early November.

Horace Ellis "Sally" Crouch, left – second row, was the only Columbian to fly the hazardous Doolittle Raid.
Photo Courtesy Martin Crouch

Horace "Sally" Crouch

1918-2005 – (Legacy Account, Martin Crouch) was the only Columbian, and one of three South Carolinians to participate in Col. Jimmy Doolittle's daring Tokyo raid. When his squadron, based in Pendleton, Oregon, received orders to report to Lexington County Airport, Crouch was taken by surprise; when he had left Columbia for Oregon, there had been no airport.

"My dad had served in the South Carolina National Guard beginning as a Citadel cadet in 1937. He entered the Army Air Corps following his 1940 graduation with a degree in Civil Engineering and accepted a commission as Second Lieutenant July 11, 1940. He became Triple Rated by attending bombardier, navigator and radar training. His honeymoon to Mount Hood, Oregon, was interrupted by Pearl Harbor. Assigned to the 89th Reconnaissance Squadron of the 17th Bombardment Group as a navigator/bombardier, he was back in his hometown when he joined 79 other volunteers for the highly-classified mission that became the Doolittle Raid."

Crouch remained in service after the war and served three tours in the Pacific and one tour each in England, North Africa, and Germany. He retired as Lieutenant Colonel on April 30, 1962. His decorations include the Silver Star, Distinguished Flying Cross, Air Medal with 1 Oak Leaf Cluster, and the Chinese Army, Navy, Air Corps Medal, Class A, 1st Grade. After retiring from his military career, he taught mathematics at Columbia High School, Columbia S.C.

Joe Bouknight, who grew up on Elmwood Avenue, made Columbia's YMCA his after school stop nearly every day, from his years at Wardlaw Elementary School through Columbia High School. One unforgettable afternoon, he was surprised to see the old gym floor full.

"When I got closer, I realized they were military – they were in khaki gym shorts and they were in great physical shape. They were being instructed to climb this rope, two or three inches thick. They had to pull all the way to the top, touch the ceiling, and come back down it. They also did regular calisthenics, worked out with weight pulleys, jumped rope, and ran the track on the second floor. I asked Jeep Rogers who they were."

Rogers, who later became Y director, a position he held for many years, told Bouknight they had been brought in for this physical training from the Lexington County Airport. "I guess from newsreels and magazine pictures, Jeep recognized Jimmy Doolittle, who was running their training session himself. This made quite an impression on a kid my age, then about 10 or 11 years old. After the Tokyo Raid, we put it all together and realized they had been the Doolittle Raiders, training right there in our Y."

Jobe Roof – Legacy Account – had for many years been farming land that became Columbia Army Air Base. Because the property take-over also took his livelihood, he was offered some sort of employment. He supervised the maintenance crew of the POW mess hall. He passed along these stories to his family. Jimmy Roof's granddaughter Anna Wilkerson used her interview with her grandfather in a school report. "My grandfather (Jimmy

Roof) saw Jimmy Doolittle crack open hickory nuts with his teeth. This greatly fascinated the young boy." Like all residing in homes on the base periphery, members of the Roof family – especially the children – were terrified by much of what was going on around them. "They never knew when a prisoner might come into their yards – some of our relatives had them come up on their porches. My granddaddy remembered hiding under his bed, his sister crying, because they were so frightened." What had been back yard play areas became the German POW camp and also an area where a fake airbase was built. "They had wooden airplanes with camouflaged covers so if any enemy planes went over, they would be confused as to where the real airport was," Wilkerson reported.

Fake jeep.
Photo by Bill Hamson

One of the discoveries the curious neighborhood children found was the prisoner of war camp. "It was practically in my grandpa's backyard; more than 200 prisoners were held there. They had an electric chair made between two pines trees, with a board for a seat. They wrapped chicken wire around the seat. They had an old telephone that they wound up, and it gave an electrical shock, enough to hurt the prisoners but not enough to kill them. They used this when the prisoners tried to escape."

Melva Craft (Hoover).
Courtesy Hoover collection

Melva Craft Hoover broke her teaching contract to do the patriotic thing: take on a job working 14 hours a day on the line. "I was putting rubber nuts on airplanes that were headed to North Africa. In that climate and under those conditions, sand would have played havoc with metal nuts and bolts. When I'd get home at night and try to get some sleep, my muscles would be so tired, they contracted all night, just about jerking me out of bed." She had just about come to the conclusion she'd made a mistake and was considering trying to go back to teaching. "But then someone high on the chain of command discovered I had teaching credentials, sent for me and asked me to teach mandatory supervisory training classes. One day a general, on base to review all operations, sat in on my class," recalled Hoover, who returned to teaching after the war, retiring in Swansea after a long career. "All students were given little cards filled with supervisory reminders. When I asked the students to get theirs out, the general got his out, too. He had taken the same training on another base, at another time." Hoover also edited a newsletter that circulated on the base.

Bobby Douglas (legacy account) recalls stories from his father, an electrician before the war broke out. "During the war he oversaw a work detail comprised of German POWs held close to base. He took them around to do various jobs and took them back at the end of each workday. The prison camp was behind the site of Airport High School."

Tom Fincher was enjoying a warm weather recess at Dutch Fork Elementary School back in 1944 when a B-25 flew over the school.

"Nothing unusual," said the author of **No Ordinary Lives: The Life and Times of Chapin Area World War II Veterans**. "We were used to seeing and hearing the bombers coming over the school; they were training over Lake Murray, just down the road. But this time was different," recalled Fincher, a fourth grader at the time.

"Our principal was standing next to me on the playground and I said to him, 'Look at the tricks that plane is doing.'" The Mitchell bomber had turned upside down, righted itself, then began spiraling out of control. Seconds later the children heard the explosion. The plane had crashed no more than a quarter mile from the school.

"Immediately, our teachers ushered us back inside the schoolhouse where they did something teachers today can't do – they led us in a prayer for the airmen who had to have perished in such a crash, such an explosion. I had nightmares about it for a long time," Fincher recalled.

Another memory from that era was of being out with his father at dawn. The wind was blowing just right. "My father asked, 'Can you hear that?' I said it sounded like a train. He said, 'It's the bombers cranking up. The way the wind is blowing, we can hear them out here in Ballentine, from all the way over at the air base. In about 20 minutes they will be flying overhead.' And sure enough, they were."

Fincher's parents had him in tow another time when they went to meet some friends serving in the Army Air Force who were having an evening out at the Skyline Club. "This was a club out in the vicinity of the airport, and that evening we walked into a smoke-filled place packed with pilots and other crewmen having a great time. They knew they would be shipping out any day, any hour, and they were living it up!"

Fincher recalls going into the old WWII hangar (next to the present-day South Carolina Aeronautics Hangar) where he saw a yellow bi-wing and other exciting planes. "Such memories inspired me to sign on for military service when I was of age," said Fincher, who retired from the U.S. Army at the rank of colonel.

Bunny Brooks found that being a good fit was perhaps her most significant contributions to the war effort. She was so petite she could get down into the wing of the B-25s, recalled the former riveter, now residing in the Blythewood area.

"Sometimes they would forget I was down in there, and the heat from the blowtorch would come way too close. One time the heat burned right through the leg of my white coverall." She shook it off and kept working.

Brooks was one of dozens of women working on Columbia Army Air

Base who could have been called, generically, Rosie the Riveter.

"One of my proudest memories is that we worked on the commander's plane."

Bill Hamson knew his way around a dark room, and his aptitude with cameras factored into the Massachusetts native's successful application for photography school after enlisting in the army in Boston soon after the war began. His previous photographic experience? Taking pictures for fun around his high school. From Fort Devens, Massachusetts, he was sent to Miami, Florida, for basic training. Hamson recalled being shown movies of enemy aircraft, then being tested to see if he recognized them. After many more tests, he qualified for technical schooling. "Then I was in the Air Force. I went into a big theater where there were lists of specialty schools I could sign up for. I put photography school as my first choice. The sergeant said my testing showed I was a little weak in math and suggested I should stay there and take some extra courses. I said, "Sergeant, you could keep me here until the end of the war and I wouldn't do any better in math,' Hamson responded. "I recommend you for photography school," the sergeant replied. Hamson was sent to Lowry Field in Denver, Colorado, and cleared requirements there before being deployed to Columbia Army Air Base.

Bill Hamson (center, back row) with his graduating class before shipping out from Lowry Field, Denver, Colorado for Columbia Army Air Base.

This is where Hamson developed pictures when he first arrived at CAAB.
Photo by Bill Hamson

For his earliest weeks on base, the photographic detail operated out of a hastily thrown up tent and trailer. Before he'd had time to settle in, he received new orders to return to Lowry for additional training, this time to learn how to process gun camera film. When he completed that, he returned to CAAB and was put on a regular training schedule.

"Each squadron has its own photography crew. I was assigned to the 426th bombardment squadron (medium). My primary job was to photograph bomb drops on training missions. Our pictures provided study aids for assessment and improvement. We printed up the pictures in a field lab, and gunnery officers led crewmen in studying them to learn what they did right, what they did wrong," said Hamson, who often was able to get off stunning aerial shots of planes in formation.

"For missions where capturing photographs was the primary purpose, cameras were mounted onto guns."

"When we flew training missions over Myrtle Beach, one crew would tow a target behind a plane while another crew shot at it. Each gunner would shoot a different color so their gunnery officers could tell who was missing the target, and by how much."

And when dignitaries, top brass or celebrities were on base, Hamson was among the photographers assigned to take those official pictures.

Being assigned to a base that, for much of the war, was hopping around the clock, 24/7, it was rare for Hamson to have time off to explore the Capital

A day away from base and a chance to swim at Sesquicentennial Park was a real treat for airmen at CAAB.
Photo by Bill Hamson

Hamson used his off-duty time to take pictures.

City he'd been sent to. But when he did, he always had a camera with him. He photographed the State House and its surroundings. On rarer forays he and buddies got out to Sesquicentennial Park in northeast Columbia.

Dan Rossman is still flying, 70 years later, only now the planes are smaller.
Photo Courtesy the Rossman Collection

Dan Rossman recalled: "Before making my first – and what I figured would be my only – trip to Columbia, South Carolina, I had to get the map out just to see where it was.

After graduating pilot training in March '44, and a 15-day leave, plus allowance for travel time, I was to report to the Columbia Army Air Base. From Washington, D.C. to Columbia, there was standing room only on standard passenger train. When I got off at the train station, I hopped a 2 X 2 truck with a sign on the side saying Columbia Army Air Base. That's how we got out to the base.

Except for the bases to which I'd been assigned for basic and advanced training, I had not ventured out of Philadelphia, my hometown, other than short trips to Atlantic City and New York. I had no preconceived notions about what a Southern town would be like and, frankly, doubted it would make any difference anyway. I had seen very little of the towns I'd been in for other trainings – Miami Beach, San Antonio and Akron/Kent State, so I didn't think I'd be seeing much of Columbia either.

I reported to the CAAFB Replacement Depot, as ordered, to await further assignment, expecting to go from Columbia to Charlotte for A-20 training. This is what I'd requested, and this is what I'd been told to expect.

My initial visit was longer than I'd anticipated, and there was little for me to do there but wait. I was assigned to what we called the ReplDepot – Replacement Depot, what amounted to a tarpaper shack, hastily thrown up. That's where I slept and took meals, usually at the PX, much closer than the Mess Hall.

As an Aviation Cadet, I was considered by the USO to be at the rank of Warrant Officer so I was not allowed in the USO – no officers were, so I never saw the inside of a USO the entire time I was in the military. I had plenty of time to go into town, but it was a chore – although I did take in a few movies and eat at a few restaurants. Because of its proximity to Fort Jackson, the city always had a great many military 'visitors', so many in fact that officers soon learned to use back streets to minimize the saluting situation. We had to salute every officer we saw; it was enough to give you tennis elbow.

One of my very few social recollections from my first stay in Columbia came about because my arm was twisted by my roommate, a bombagator (bombardier and navigator). He asked if I had anything on for tonight; I said, "Are you kidding?" He talked me into going out with him and a girlfriend. I met some very nice young ladies, and we had a good time.

When I finally got my orders, they were to report to Greenville, South Carolina, where I was to continue my training in a B-25 – here I was on a huge B-25 base, and they wanted me to go to a different B-25 base. When I left, my roommate still had no idea where he was going. I lost contact with him, so I never found out.

My overall recollection of Columbia? As anxious as I was to 'get on with it', I thoroughly enjoyed my six week stay in Columbia. I certainly never expected to come back, but I have many times, and I've liked every Columbian I've met on my numerous returns to the city since March 1944. As a born-and-raised-in-Philadelphia Northerner, Columbia was the first Southern city I encountered and it set a standard hard to beat.

Alvin Strasburger, at age 17, had just completed his first semester at Clemson College when the Japanese bombed Pearl Harbor and the U.S. entered WWII. Clemson was a military school then, so he already had been marching with a rifle and had even been chosen to join the crack drill team

(The Pershing Rifles) that performed at half-time during football games. He joined the Army Air Corps Reserves in March 1942 and was called to active duty in January 1943. He was sent to Miami Beach, Florida, for basic training. "What did they want to teach me? How to march, carry a rifle - and discipline!" Things were so crowded then they didn't have room for him when he finished basic training, so he was sent to Kutztown State Teachers College in Pennsylvania, between Allentown and Reading, for about six weeks. After that he was sent to Randolph Field, Texas, where he was placed into pilot training. There were several more places for pilot training (basic and advanced) and Houston, Texas. After six weeks training in twin engine aircraft, one morning in January 1944, he went to the bulletin board, and by A. Strasburger's name was: Replacement Depot, Columbia Army Air Base. They put wings on his shoulders and made him a Second Lieutenant.

When he got back to Columbia, he stayed at home with his mother and father and went out to the Columbia Army Air Base every morning. He was flying as a co-pilot. "The B-25 was a great plane." By late August or early September, he was on a ship out of Norfolk, Virginia, on the way to Naples, Italy. He was then flown to Corsica where the 25s were located. When he had about ten missions, he was promoted to First Lieutenant and first pilot, "then I flew about 50 missions over the Po Valley and the Brenner Pass bombing railroad bridges and supply depots. The Brenner Pass connected Italy and Germany through Austria."

On his 41st mission, he lost the right engine and had a fire on board. He had some shrapnel come through his seat and into his right leg, close to his groin. "After putting out the fire, we had to fly on one engine to Florence, Italy." He later received the DSC for that mission. "In 1945 our squadron was transferred to Rimini, Italy, on the Adriatic Sea. I flew the rest of my 60 missions from there. On May 23 1945, my 21st birthday, I got orders to return to the USA. When I got to New Jersey, they told me I had enough points to get out of the Army Air Corp." He replied "I'll take that".

"Instead of returning to Clemson, I went to Yale and finished my BA degree. I then went for a semester to Columbia University before deciding I'd had enough school. I came back to Columbia and went into business with my father."

Strasburger enjoyed reuniting with members of his bomb group when they met at Adam's Mark Hotel (now Marriott again) in Columbia in September 1992. "I think I only recognized one guy from the group, Hal

Lynch. Hal had been a bombardier and a prisoner of war. I had renewed our friendship while I was at Yale. Hal reintroduced me to Col Kaufman, who I had thought was much older than I because of his rank, but we were not that far apart."

Murray Price recalls that in the early 1940s, throughout the South Carolina Midlands, the early morning thrumming of B-25s was a more certain wake-up call than any rooster could produce. "When they started cranking up those engines, you could hear them all the way to Columbia where my family lived at the time; I was told you could hear them in Lexington, and if the wind was right, as far away as Eastover," recalled Murray Price. The sounds admonished the young man it was time to get up. Duty was calling.

The civil servant reported weekdays to Columbia's main post office location, across from the State House, where he sorted and slotted mail. But on or near paydays, he was sent out to the new Lexington County Airport to help at the base post office with the stepped up demand for money orders. "Servicemen were good about sending money home," recalled Price, who caught aviation fever, just from being on the training base. "I would look up and see those planes taking off, coming in. I am sure that's what influenced me to apply to the Aviation Cadet program."

Price was accepted and began a series of training that took him to the American West, although he did not see many of the sights beyond the confines of the air bases. None of his orders brought him back to Columbia Army Air Base – the plane that became second nature to him was a B-24, not a B-25.

He was only on his fifth mission, target: Iwo Jima, when the B-24 he was co-piloting in a twelve-bomber formation came under Japanese Zeros' attack. The enemy disabled the plane on Price's immediate right within the formation, and when the compromised aircraft was separated from its formation, the Japanese blew it to bits. The Zeroes did not relent, even with fire coming at them from American turrets and tails. Miraculously, the remaining eleven bombers made it to their target zone and dropped the munitions as ordered.

Following that mission Price became the pilot of that shaken crew, but in spite of other close calls, no member of Price's crew was wounded or killed. For their various actions during service, all crew members were awarded the Distinguished Flying Cross and the Air Medal with six Oak Leaf Clusters.

When he had completed forty combat missions, Price returned state side in May 1945. The homecoming was bittersweet. He has repeated in interviews over the years: "Some of us who were whole and well felt a bit embarrassed, like we really didn't belong there after watching disabled vets moving down the gangplank. I still remember the extreme joy and deep sadness, rolled together. There were tears in my eyes and a lump in my throat."

When he made it home that August 1945, he became better acquainted with the hometown girl he married in June 1946. While he was up in the "wild blue yonder", often over Saipan and Guam, Frances Addy had been doing her part to stoke morale at Columbia Army Air Base. "She rarely missed one of the dances," Price said. "The USO would have girls picked up and driven out to wherever on base the dances were to be. She rode in the back of a truck in evening dresses. She was such a "regular" she became friends with members of the band."

Lynn Mascall Geis (Legacy Account)

Note: This legacy account is taken from the public address Lynn Mascall Geis gave at the unveiling of an historic marker at Lake Murray Sunday, April 19, 2009, the final day of the 67th annual Doolittle Raiders' Reunion – the third time the momentous occasion was held in Columbia.

The scene here today could not have been imagined on that April day in 1943 when my father and the rest of the B 25 crew ditched in this lake. I was born at the base hospital in August of that year, and today I stand here with grey hair, wearing daddy's wedding ring – a ring that was on his finger that day. I'm here to honor the memory of my father and the many other men to whom this marker is dedicated.

What were all the forces of imagination and dedication that motivated Dr Robert Seigler to persist for so many years in his effort to bring that plane back to the light of day? Any explanation I read fails to capture the passion of the endeavor. When he contacted my parents 14 years ago, they experienced many emotions: surprise, excitement, incredulity. In what turned out to be the last decade of their lives, they enjoyed the attention brought to them from this early chapter of their lives.

At the time of the salvage project, Rachel Haynie and Kay Gordon contacted my folks to get a few anecdotes to flesh out human-interest stories about a young couple's wartime experiences in Columbia. Rachel found herself being drawn more and more into a story that she thought could illuminate a particular slice of Columbia history. Three years ago she came to Portland to meet my parents, I picked her up at her hotel, and we have stayed in touch ever since as she has expanded that original article into a full-length narrative of wartime Columbia – with my parents as the main characters. What an amazing turn of events for our family!

Both of my parents came from Oregon pioneer families. They grew up in very small towns – population less than 500. They met at a summer dance when mom was 15, dad a 19 year old college man. Four years later, with the country at war, dad enlisted in the Army Air Corps. At the end of the training, he asked his sweetheart to come to Midland, Texas, to pin his wings on, and they made a spontaneous decision to get married. Three days later Mom headed back to Oregon and Dad came to Columbia. Once here he discovered a permission existed that would clear him to live off base, and that some other airmen's wives were here, he wrote her to come as soon as possible. So she got back on a train and headed to Columbia. About nine months later, I was born at the hospital on the base.

When Lynn Mascall Geis' father, Hank Mascall, received new orders to leave CAAB and report to Florida, mother Gerry (left) and baby daughter Mary Lynn visited the beach nearby.
Courtesy Mascall collection

In spite of the awesome seriousness of the times, it was a grand adventure for these two small town kids. Growing up, I heard about the crash, and lived with Dad's back troubles that set him up for three surgeries over the next dozen years. But that was all downplayed. They liked to tell how Dad left his nearly new $17 hat in the plane, and that when he came home that day without it, any idea that he would keep the crash a secret from his pregnant wife was quickly scuttled.

I heard more about friends they made and life in the South. Some of the stories were about Mom trying to learn what a proper southern housewife should do. For example, she shouldn't buy a live chicken, wring its neck and pluck it herself. She shouldn't jack up a car and change a flat. I guess her landlady was scandalized.

I am honored to be here as my father's representative to thank Dr. Seigler and Rachel Haynie and all the many other people I'll never meet. My parents lived to see the Mega Movers program that documented the salvage

Lynn Mascall Geis, foreground, with her husband Ed Geis, Dr. Bill Vartorella and Dr. Robert Seigler participated in the historical marker unveiling ceremony at Lake Murray as the 67th annual Doolittle Raiders Reunion drew to a close.
Author photo

effort and enjoyed the attention that brought them. They were amazed that so many people were determined to bring up the plane, but fascinated by the project. I have to say, the high point for them was the discovery that his hat brim had survived over sixty years of underwater storage.

Dad died just after Christmas of 2006, and Mom died just 3 months later, two days after Easter. They would be deeply touched to know about this dedication and would be thrilled that I was able to be here. I am deeply touched by this experience. I am one of five children and I know some of my siblings, our kids or nieces and nephews will make their way to Columbia or Birmingham (Alabama, where the B-25 is on exhibit at the Southern Museum of Flight) one of these days. They would love to see this area and Dad's plane for themselves.

Harold Jones recalls much of Columbia Army Air Base's history from his early years, growing up near the complex. His family lived on Frink Street in West Columbia. "I remember as a boy going down by the railroad tracks, picking up chunks of coal that rumbled off the train cars coming through on the tracks that ran near our homes. Trains came through there often, taking materials and supplies to the airbase. If coal fell off, we'd gather it up and take it home to burn in our stoves."

Still just a young boy, Jones got his start in business selling the local newspaper out at Fort Jackson in the afternoons. Some years after the war ended, he established a business on part of the former base; with Gary P. Smith he founded Smith and Jones Antique Auto Parts in a former military building that remained on property after the government designated most of the base as surplus. Being

Harold Jones knows the former air base well; the business he has run for many years is headquartered in a building that had been part of the facility.
Author photo

on the very site of the former base, he learned the terrain well. On his own time, in his own vehicle, using his own fuel, he has given countless informal tours of the former base, pointing out the few remnants still visible. In 2010 he discovered and refurbished the site where the base headquarters' flagpole stood during WWII, then led the charge to rededicate it in a patriotic flag-raising ceremony hosted December 5, 2010, by the South Carolina Historic Aviation Foundation. The community event also marked the beginning of the 70 anniversary of the property's transfer from private farm owners to the federal government. In 1940 development began for the facility initially named Lexington County Airport; until The Day of Infamy (the attack on Pearl Harbor), the airport was projected to serve as a commercial enterprise. More recently, Jones has led a new charge: to find and compile names of more than 250 airmen who perished in training accidents while serving at CAAB. Plans are for those names to be etched into black granite and become the central element in a monument to the memory of those courageous airmen. The monument is to be designed, executed and installed by Memorial Design, Ron and Sallie Clamp of Stonecrafters Farm.

Johnson Miles Irwin was a gunner assigned to Columbia Army Air Base in the mid-40s. "I spent much of my flying time in a top turret," said the recently-retired businessman from Grand Rapids, Michigan. He refreshed his recollections of that part of his past on a recent return to Columbia en route to Florida with son David Irwin. "I had been working in a Cadillac factory that was making airplane engines for Allison just before I entered service at Ft. Custer (Michigan). I was ordered to Columbia when I completed training in Miami." Irwin was stationed at CAAB long enough to be joined by his wife and infant son. He later was deployed to the South Pacific theatre where one of his most memorable brushes with history involved crewing on a B-25 escorting Japanese planes to and from Ieshima at the time of the surrender. The father and son were traveling to Florida from Michigan in early November and stopped to see the rare B-25C in the stewardship of the South Carolina Historic Aviation Foundation.

Leroy McKinney, an MP guarding German prisoners at Columbia Army Air Base, was ordered to retrieve the prisoners from their work detail – the mess hall kitchen - and return them to their compound early one September morning in 1945. News was breaking around the world – Japan had surrendered. The war was over.

"I guess Americans were afraid when the Germans heard the news, there would be a riot or something, but they were as happy to hear the war was over as we were. Only, they did not want to go back to Germany," recalled McKinney, who had been moved from Fort Jackson for this highly-volatile guard duty.

McKinney learned no German from his prisoners, but both sides figured out some ways to communicate. "Sometimes they would offer us gifts; we couldn't figure out where they were getting them, where they could have been keeping them, because we inspected their barracks regularly to make sure they didn't have anything dangerous. But they might come up with a bottle of perfume or something, saying, 'Take this to your wife.'" For McKinney, that was Lula Estelle, a girl he met while serving at CAAB. They have been married 67 years.

"We would pick them up and take them to their work detail which was often the mess hall or maybe work in pulp wood, as far off as Camden. So, by day they had a guard with them at all times. At night we guarded them from towers on all four corners of their compound. "The prisoners usually didn't give us any problems," McKinney recalled.

"I do remember one incident. They had a soccer field about where Airport High School is today and they were playing a game one day when a prisoner called another guard a bad name. Well, Grady Cooper was a hot-tempered Tennessee mountain fellow. He emptied his carbine, sent several of them to the hospital. He was fined $1, a carton of cigarettes, and was discharged."

After the war the prisoners were moved to Fort Jackson and, from there, on a series of maneuvers before they reached New Jersey from where they were shipped back to Germany. "They sure did not want to go," McKinney said.

Tina Palasis Leventis worried, knowing her delivery time was nearing. Her husband Peter had been recuperating from war injuries at Columbia Army Air Base hospital, but the war had ended and the hospital was to close. Where would she have this baby? Her husband, understanding military protocol, talked doctors into keeping the hospital open just a few more days. Her son Phil (now South Carolina Senator Phil Leventis) was born November 3, 1945, one of the last babies delivered before operations at the base hospital ceased.

Donald Edwin White flew first in the Royal Canadian Air Force before switching to the U.S. Army Air. He already was a highly decorated pilot before receiving orders to report to Columbia Army Air Base May 14, 1945. "As long as the war in the Pacific was still raging, pilots needed to maintain proficiency, especially low-level flying, so we flew missions over Lake Murray." While on base he also did some boxing. When the war ended, he ferried B-25s from CAAB to Peru and helped train Peruvian Air Force pilots.

(Dr.) James Steele was based at CAAB for only 28 days before being shipped out for other duty, but that was long enough for the navigator to calibrate a few compasses, take a few training missions over Lake Murray, and meet and marry Marie Terry. He completed his education following the war and practiced general medicine in Lexington, SC. He and Marie celebrated their 67th wedding anniversary in November 2011.

Charles Shealy, tailgunner, was surprised to receive orders to return to Columbia, his hometown, following training in Miami and Ft. Myers, Florida. "Mostly, we flew night missions, practicing bombing over Lake Murray." Because he was from Columbia, he was allowed to live off base, which suited the newlywed very well.

Wilfred G. Janes (Legacy Account, Louise Riley) was a senior aircraft welder and supervisor on Columbia Army Air Base. On Family Visitors' Day, he showed his wife and young daughter around, even pointing out camouflaged planes scattered about in the woods behind the base. To give his daughter a sense of what it felt like to parachute out of a plane, he had Louise stand at the bay while he yelled, "Bombs Away! She recalled the ground seeming a long way down from the edge of the bomb bay. "But I jumped," said Riley, of Leesville "I can still feel the thrill as I moved through the air to my dad's outstretched arms – he caught me!"

Carl Carter Chambers (Legacy Account, Nancy Chambers Beaver), an engineer on Columbia Army Air Base, entered military service shortly after earning his engineering degree from Purdue University where he met Anne Anderson, his future wife. The newlyweds lived off base in Columbia's

Shandon neighborhood and their daughter, Nancy, was born in the base hospital October 26, 1944."My mother never knew when he would have to leave, or for how long," said Beaver, again a Columbia resident.

Claude Redmond (Legacy Account, Leo Redmond, curator of Cayce Historical Museum) served as a civilian fireman on base. "All the firemen, on call 24 hours a day, took turns cooking for the entire crew. They looked forward to my dad's turn because he was the best cook. His specialty was steak and gravy."

CHAPTER FIFTEEN

> I have returned many times to honour the valiant men who died...every man who set foot on Omaha Beach was a hero.
>
> > Lieutenant General Omar Bradley
> > Commander of the US First Army
> > (Speaking after the war)

CHAPTER FIFTEEN

After the War

Training at CAAB was phased down during the summer of 1945. During September and October, several units arrived from overseas to inactivate.

With the end of WWII, the base experienced a massive demobilization of personnel and inactivation of units that lasted through April 1946.

Included in those departing the base were the German POWs. One German POW in particular had earned the trust – and even friendship – of Jobe Roof, the farmer whose land had been absorbed into the base, and whose job it had been to oversee aspects of the POWs activities. The German who became Roof's friend begged the former farmer to keep him, to allow him to stay and live with him in America; however, that was not possible according to the terms of the German's surrender in Europe. All the POWs were sent back.

But before the German POWs left, there was sweeping festivity in the neighborhood surrounding the base. Celebrating were the families who had lived in such fear throughout the war – fear a plane would crash into their yards, which happened, or that a German POW would escape and encroach, come up on their porches, hoping for entry, for sanctuary, which also happened. The war was over and the POWs were included in a party for which fifty pigs were barbequed.

In accordance with the government's promise, Jobe Roof was given a new job so that he could earn a living for his family. From 30 April 1946 to 5 April 1947, the based was on stand-by status, then later was used as a training facility, home of the 350th Bombardment Squadron of the U.S. Air Force Reserve.

On 27 June 1949, CAAB was declared surplus to the needs of the U.S. Air Force and was made available for commercial aviation. Government-acquired land reverted to Lexington County.

Up to that time, all airline operations had been being accommodated at Owens Field in Columbia. Shortly thereafter, a terminal was established at the Lexington County facility. The terminal building constructed at the Lexington County Airport in the early 1950s burned; another one was quickly built and used until the present terminal opened in 1965. (Note: A major terminal renovation was completed in 1997.)

General Doolittle returned to Columbia in May, 1980, for the dedication of a U.S. Army Aviation Flight Facility named for him. Its location? The site from which he invited volunteers for the historic mission that took his name. Only, by the early '80s, the airfield had become Columbia Metropolitan Airport.

The importance of Lake Murray, during war years a liquid training strip, as a leisure destination was captured in 1973 by Coy Bayne in his initial release of **Lake Murray: Legend and Leisure**. When he re-released it in 1992, his new cover wore a reproduction of artist Jamie Blackburn's surreal painting depicting one of the lost B-25s resting on the lake floor. In Russell Maxey's1987 release, **Airports of Columbia: A History in Photographs and Headlines**, the photographer and historian who had been ordered to paint white lines on the runway to facilitate short-run take-offs, also referred to B-25s that had gone into the lake during the war years' training missions.

Later in the 20th century, underwater diving had grown as a hobby, so that exploration was possible regarding the disappearance of B-25s into Lake Murray. Rumors regarding how many bombers were "down there" could finally be refuted with technological advances, including SONAR. The stories added mystique to the body of water over which CAAB airmen trained during WWII.

But Lake Murray was not the only watery landing strip on which WWII-era planes ditched during WWII. Less than 75 miles away, an aircraft that had begun its service record in Columbia, then had been borrowed by the air base in Greenville, ditched into Lake Greenwood on a routine training mission on D-Day.

Considered unsalvageable at the time because of the water depth into which the plane sank, the aircraft spent 39 years on the lake floor. Then in 1983 rescue efforts led by Greenwood businessman Mat Self gave the plane a new lease, a new day. The rare Mitchell bomber surfaced, filled with mud and debris, and was brought out of Lake Greenwood by teams of divers and other rescue specialists.

The aircraft was on dry land once again, nearly four decades after it sank.

The legend surrounding the plane captured the attention of civilians and military personnel, military historians and curiosity seekers.

The plane's destiny had been charted by an unfortunate training mistake. On that early June day, while practicing low-level bombing runs over Lake Greenwood, the instructor pilot swooped a little too low, and when a propeller touched the water, the plane was disabled; the instructor pilot had to ditch, and the aircraft sank in minutes. There were no serious crew injuries, but the plane was lost under water and, shortly afterwards, was declared unrecoverable by the Army Air Force.

Although the rescue effort magnetized a flurry of media attention, no entity stepped forward to undertake a restoration of the plane – as Self had expected.

The B-25 rescued from Lake Greenwood sat, forlorn, for more years before it finally was transported to Columbia where it has undergone some attempts at restoration over the years.
Photo courtesy of South Carolina Historic Aviation Foundation

So, after 39 years lost under the waters of Lake Greenwood, the plane still was without sponsorship. It sat, drying out, on the runway of the Greenwood County Airport for quite a while. From that point forward, the plane passed through a succession of owner groups, and ultimately was returned to Columbia, specifically to the historic Curtiss Wright Hangar at Owens Airport.

In readying the plane to serve as a rallying point for the 1992 Doolittle

Raiders Reunion to be hosted in Columbia by the City of Columbia, the iconic plane – a singular representative of the service that radiated from CAAB to combat zones in war theaters around the globe – received modified restorations.

Photo courtesy South Carolina Historic Aviation Foundation

The surviving Raiders so enjoyed being back in the city where it all began for their 50th reunion – where they were wined, dined, transported in vintage cars, saluted and honored – the storied aviation heroes returned in 2002 for their 60th, and in 2009 for their 67th historic gathering.

The Doolittle Raiders returned to Columbia in 1992 for their 50th annual reunion. Photo courtesy of South Carolina Historic Aviation Foundation

Vintage cars conveyed the Doolittle Raiders along their parade route.
Photo by author

When they returned to Columbia in 2002, the Raiders heard rumblings about plans a Columbia native, by then a pediatric specialist practicing in Greenville, was making to lead the rescue of the B-25C that had ditched into Lake Murray in April 1943. For years the efforts of Dr. Robert Sanders Seigler and others comprising the Lake Murray B-25 Rescue Group were beset with myriad slowdowns, hitches, even foul weather conditions on the scheduled rescue day.

But four years before the Raiders held their 67th reunion in Columbia – 2009 – the aircraft known as the Lake Murray Bomber had surfaced and been trucked to the Southern Museum of Flight in Birmingham, Alabama.

Seigler, who had water-skied on the lake as a youth, could

Dr. Robert Seigler (left) brought in world-famous vintage airplane salver Gary Larkins to insure success of the B-25s rescue.
Photo courtesy of Dr. Warner Montgomery

scarcely remember a time he had not heard lore and rumors about WWII planes that had gone into the drink. His quest to see that one fabled plane recovered from 150 feet of water spanned more than a decade. For his successful efforts he was named Lake Murray Association's Man of the Year in 2006.

The association meeting at which Seigler accepted the honor also featured Dr. Jim Griffin, director of Southern Museum of Aviation in Birmingham, Alabama, who described for the audience the process the aircraft had experienced since its recovery and transfer to the museum.

Griffin explained that the condition of the rescued plane would have made full restoration "nearly a duplication. To make it look like it looked in 1943, we would have had to replace more than 90 percent of the plane. In its exhibit space, the plane is being viewed as a time capsule. Visitors can better envision what its 60 years on the bottom of the lake did to it than they would if the plane was made to look new," Griffin explained.

While this relic and reminder of the contributions made by personnel at CAAB had left the state, the aircraft known as the Lake Greenwood B-25 retained its Columbia address. For many years it was in the stewardship of Celebrate Freedom Foundation whose mission is to educate the public, especially school children. The foundation hosts programming that honors those who have served this nation in the defense of freedom and liberty, both past and present, and to promote lasting American patriotism.

But late in 2010, that foundation had plans to remove the B-25 from its inventory. A group of historic and civic minded individuals learned that the plane was set to be sold to an out-of-state interest. Forming quickly as the South Carolina Historic Aviation Foundation (SCHAF), the group intervened, purchased the plane and became its steward. Assessments regarding fundamental restoration efforts began immediately, along with fundraising efforts and a membership drive. The patriotic group was responsive when a friend of CAAB made an unexpected find.

From time to time, business Harold Jones, with headquarters in a building that was part of the base facilities during WWII, had given informal tours to former CAAB servicemen and/or their families, pointing out the few remnants from the early '40s. Well familiar with the physical characteristics of the area, he still was surprised when he unearthed what he believed to be the site of the base post headquarters' flagpole. On his own he cleaned, then refurbished the raised concrete area, and brought the historic discovery to the attention of the South Carolina Historic Aviation Foundation (SCHAF). The newly-formed organization spearheaded a re-dedication of the flagpole in a patriotic ceremony Sunday, December 12.

At that cold December event, SCHAF President Cantzon Foster announced the organization would lead, in December 2011, a public commemoration of the 70th anniversary of CAAB's opening.

As the December 3 date approached, myriad individuals and families touched by the presence of the air base have been reunited through various forms of communication. Although the base closed before the end of the 40's decade, its affect can still be felt throughout the Midlands and beyond by those who passed through its gates.

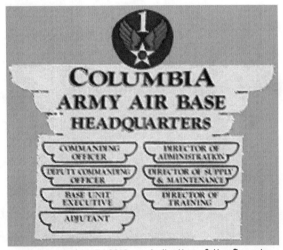

For the December 5, 2010 re-dedication of the flagpole that had punctuated conspicuous space outside the base commander's headquarters, businessman Harold Jones had a local sign company re-create the signage used outside headquarters.
Photo by author

The flagpole plaza that, during the Columbia Army Air Base service years was adjacent to base headquarters, was rediscovered, refurbished, and the site re-dedicated on December 5, 2010, in a brief ceremony hosted by the South Carolina Historic Aviation Foundation. Recognized during the event was Harold Jones, the businessman and citizen patriot who undertook the recovery and restoration. He sees that the American flag goes up that pole every day.
Photo by Ron Shelton

BASE COMMANDERS

U.S. Army Air Forces
Columbia Army Air Base

8 December 1941	24 December 1941	Lt. Col. Dache M. Reeves (Owens Field)
31 December 1941	1 April 1944	Lt. Col. William G. Murphy (CEO)
2 January 1942	8 January 1944	Col. William. B. Mayer (Hospitalized)
8 January 1942	18 January 1942	Capt. John J. Kennedy (Temporary)
18 January 1942	6 April 1942	Col. William B. Mayer (Returns)
April 1942	12 October 1942	Col. Gilbert T. Collar (Daniel Field)
12 October 1943	25 November 1945	Col. Guy L. McNeil
25 November		Col. Daniel W. Jenkins

PRINCIPLE UNITS
Stationed At Columbia Army Air Base
1941-1949

8 December 1941	24 December 1941	65th Observation Group
9 November 1942	23 June 1942	17th Bombardment Group
9 February 1932	December 1942	312th Service Group
10 February 1942	1 May 1942	96th Base HQ and Air Base Squadron
21 February 1942	20 May 1942	19th Air Base Group
2 March 1942	19 October 1942	320th Service Group
2 March 1942`	14 September 1942	319th Service Group
21 April 1942	24 May 1942	21st Bombardment Group
16 May 1942	1 May 1944	309th Bombardment Group
31 May 1942	1 May 1944	21st Sub Depot
1 August 1942	September 1942	321st Bombardment Group
4 August 1942	21 August 1942	323rd Bombardment Group
10 August 1942	1 May 1944	900th Guard Squadron

10 August 1942	6 March 1945	61st Air Force Band
20 August 1942	30 November 1942	340th Bombardment Group
8 September 1942	6 March 1943	345th Bombardment Group
14 September 1942	28 October 1942	53rd Service Group
29 October 1942	1 May 1944	339th Aviation Squadron
1 March 1943	15 April 1943	65th Observation Group (returns)
14 June 1943	30 September 1943	910th WAAC Post HQ Company
1 May 1944	31 January 1945	329th Army Air Forces Base Unit
30 January 1945	27 April 1945	514th Service Group
1 February 1945	30 April 1946	129th Army Air Forces Base Unit
28 February 1945	27 April 1945	319th Bombardment Group
16 September 1945	13 November 1945	520th Service Group
2 October 1945	7 November 1945	340th Bombardment Group (returns)
30 April 1946	5 April 1947	103 Army Air Forces Group
16 July 1947	27 June 1949	350th Bombardment Squadron (Reserves)
27 June 1949		CAAB declared surplus to needs of U.S. Air Force and made available for commercial aviation

TIMELINE OF DATES PERTINENT TO COLUMBIA ARMY AIR BASE

25 January 1939 The Army Air Corps sent out invitations to manufacturers to submit design data for a medium bombardment airplane to replace the Douglas B-18 bomber.

1 September 1939 War broke out in Europe.

17 September 1940 The U.S. instituted the first-ever peacetime draft along with a five-fold increase in the defense budget, from $2 billion to $10 billion.

December 1940 President Roosevelt proclaimed the U.S. would be the "arsenal of Democracy", and proposed selling munitions to Britain and Canada.

11 March 1941 President Roosevelt signs the Lend-Lease Bill authorizing the U.S. to supply vast amounts of war materials to the United Kingdom, the Soviet Union, China, France, and other allied nations.

8 December 1941 The airport was activated with Lt. Col. Dashe W. Reeves as commander and assigned to Third Air Force, III Air Support Command. The 121st Observation Squadron moved to the new air base from Owens Field.

10 January 1942 Captain Francis S. "Frog" Low, a submariner on the staff of Admiral Ernest J. King, hatched the idea that USAAF medium bombers might be able to take off from the deck of an aircraft carrier.

22 January, 1942 Eighteen B-25s left Wright Field for Minnesota fabrication shop for modifications according to specifications set by Lt. Col. Jimmy Doolittle.

6 February 1942 The first medical-department personnel to be stationed at the base arrived from Hunter Field, Savannah, Georgia.

9 February 1942 The 17th Bombardment Group arrived from Pendleton Field, Oregon where they had been flying antisubmarine patrols off the west coast of the United States.

17 February 1942 24 full combat crews, volunteers from the recently transferred airmen from the Oregon base, were detached from Eighth Air Force and transferred to Eglin Field, Florida to begin intensive training for an unspecified mission which later went down in history as the Doolittle Raid.

March 1942 The American Red Cross established a part-time mobile office (the back of a Red Cross truck) at the base.

2 April 1942 A letter received from the war department officially changed the name of the Lexington County Airport to Columbia Army Air Base.

6 April 1942 Col. Mayer was relieved of his command and Lt. Col. William S. Murphy assumed temporary command.

13 April 1942 Co. Gilbert T. Collar assumed command of the base.

15 April 1942 The first combat group to complete its training at the base moved out.

13 June 1942 the first entertainment band was organized on base.

28 June 1942 Walterboro, South Carolina's Anderson Airport became the first sub-base of Columbia Army Air Base, followed later that summer by sub-bases opened at airfields in Greenwood, South Carolina, and Congaree, South Carolina.

1 July 1942 First on-base newspaper, Tailspin Topics, published its first edition.

1 July 1942 A veterinary detachment was activated to advise the Base Surgeon and inspect, for quality and sanitation, all meat and dairy products to be used on base.

12 July 1942 First bond rally was held, with movie star Luise Rainer visiting the base to enhance the success of the efforts to sell war bonds. Through a payroll deduction plan introduced on the same date, service personnel could buy bonds without making a separate banking transaction.

13 July 1942 Civilian firemen took over responsibility for the pumpers and crash trucks.

14 July 1942 The first WAC detachment activated as 810th WAAC Post Headquarters Company and was welcomed under Company Commander Lt. Lelia Fay. Also on that date, the first dance was held on base.

10 August 1942 The Air Force Band was activated and redesignated a few days later as the 61st Army Air Forces Band.

October 1942 Officers moved to standard buildings, abandoning their tents. A dial telephone system was activated.

28 November 1942 The official band participated in Lexington ceremonies honoring the heroes of December 7, 1941.

4 April 1943 Under-secretary of War Robert P. Patterson inspected training facilities at the base as part of his Southern tour. He was accompanied by U.S. Sen. Burnet R. Maybank.

May 1943 Incendiary Section of the 503rd Chemical Storage Company activated.

15 July 1943 First WAC wedding: Roxie Perry married Sgt. James Mundy at the Base Chapel. The couple held the reception in the WAAC Dayroom.

26 July 1943 The Incendiary Section of the 503rd Chemical Storage Company that had been activated in May received a Warrant Officer and Staff Sergeant for the section whose purpose was to supervise the handling of toxic chemicals and ammunition.

21 August 1943 Base engineer ordered to prepare camps for German Prisoners of War to arrive in three days.

19 September 1943 A cadre of 18 foreign news correspondents cleared by the War department visited the base to study the training program, observe equipment used, and dine at Durham Hall as guests of Col. Gilbert Collar, base commander. The inquisitive guests were particularly interested in the B-25 because of its role in many headline-making strikes – from the Tokyo Raid to the North African, Sicilian, and Alaskan campaigns.

9 October 1943 An Army Air Forces Cadet Drive was held at Owens Field.

12 October 1943 Col. Guy L. McNeil assumed command of the base, following the command of Col. Gilbert Collar.

6 June 1944 D-Day.

November 1944 The arrival of 300 German POWs caused quite a stir throughout the base complex.

9 January 1945 The first A-26 arrived and immediately was put into the training schedule.

1 February 1945 the Third Air Force turned CAAB over to the First Air Force at which time the base became the 129th AAF Base Unit.

2 September 1945 Formal surrender of Japan.

KILLED IN ACTION

These airmen, and one WASP pilot, made the ultimate sacrifices while attached to, approaching or departing Columbia Army Air Base on training missions or service deliveries of aircraft. Their names enter the record books as Killed in Action.

Name and rank

2Lt George F. Hayman Jr.
1Lt A.C. Darden
Pvt C.D. Fischer
Capt James A. Plant
2Lt Howard E. Henthorn
S/Sgt Arlyn A. Gustafson
S/Sgt Louis F. Turner Jr.
Pvt Samuel A. McDonald
Pvt Frank E. Sailer
Pvt Joseph A. Schmidt
2Lt Neal Dow Curtis
2Lt Robert Roy Patillo
Pvt Floyd H. Shuman
Pvt Roy E. Graves
Pvt Benedict N. Streit
Pvt Alphie V. Took
Pvt Philip V. Downing
2Lt Francis W. Sparks
2Lt Martin O. Vangsness
2Lt Donald V. Urquhart
2Lt James Francis Attridge Jr.
Sgt Leon O. Gallie
S/Sgt Charles O. Frame
Pvt Roland G. Braun
2Lt Arnold P. Libman
2Lt Lonnie Collins Tucker Jr.
T/Sgt Bert H. Ray
S/Sgt Edward L. Davis

2nd Lt Arnold P. Libman
2nd Lt Lonnie C. Tucker JRB
TSGT Bert H. Ray
SSGT Edward T. Davis
2Lt Thomas M. Macteer
S/Sgt Peter P. Conrad
S/Sgt Alex W. Kaiser
Capt Charles T. Ceronsky
2Lt Ronald A. McDonald
S/Sgt Michael R. Poinson
2Lt Albert E. R. Broyles
2Lt Don J. Butler
2Lt John Bugra
Pfc William L. Young
S/Sgt Billy Pinkerton
S/Sgt Morris O. Jones
S/Sgt Morris Beital
Pvt Donald W. Goforth
Pvt Frank L. Good Jr.
2Lt Douglas W. Cole
2Lt Forrest E. Carter
2Lt William S. Stewart
Sgt Gene E. Lefler
2Lt William A. Johnson
2Lt Eugene L. Huntley
2Lt Charles M. Frizzell
2Lt Harold W. Hope
S/Sgt Donald W. Evans

Cpl Charles J. Miller
Pvt Vincent J. Meculskas
2Lt Carrol N. Peacock Jr.
2Lt Charles E. Hoyt Jr.
Pvt Alfred E. Brandt
Pvt Howard P. Fonville
2Lt John W. Gilluly
2Lt Leonard V. Sheffield
2Lt Edward R. Armstrong
2Lt Ross T. Morrison
2Lt Joseph F. Denning
2Lt John D. Trimmier
2Lt Robert E. Thomas
S/Sgt Lawrence F. Ford
S/Sgt Earl Fynan
Sgt Julian C. Aycock
Sgt Alton J. Jones
S/Sgt William J. Gorman
S/Sgt Jack E. Blackled
S/Sgt William F. Hosey
S/Sgt Abe Seitz
S/Sgt Forrest C. Houck
S/Sgt Jack Zelen
Sgt Alfred T. Secor
S/Sgt Jack E. Blackledge
S/Sgt W. F. Hosey
S/Sgt Jack Zelen
S/Sgt Alfred T. Secor, Jr.
S/Sgt Abe B. Seitz
S/Sgt Forest C. Houck
FST Officer Frank E. Mason
2nd Lt Lynn L. Beebe
2nd Lt Bradley O. Oliver
MSGT Milton F. Floan
PVT Cecil E. Rook
2Lt Merritt M. Hopson
2Lt Walter R. Bone
S/Sgt Vernon L. Arenas
Cpl Hal W. Reed

2Lt Merritt M. Hopson
2Lt Walter R. Bone
Cpl Hal W. Reed
S/Sgt Vernon L. Arenas
2Lt Lynn L. Beebe
2Lt Bradley C. Oliver
FO Frank E. Mason
M/Sgt Milton J. Floan
Pvt Cecil A. Rook
F/O Raymond G. Strover
F/O Warren L. Kendrick
Sgt A. J. Cairns
Sgt T. J. Connalonga
Sgt G. L. Finney
Sgt F. B. Dubois
1Lt Arnold W. Kay
2Lt Floyd A. W. Hall
S/Sgt Arnold A. Lassen
S/Sgt Roland Medlin
TSgt Roy S. Zufall
Cpl Georgia V Silva
2Lt Virgil L. Blevins
2Lt Ralph L. Knepper
2Lt Ralph F. Bladell
S/Sgt Jay G. Alms
S/Sgt Franklin McCue
S/Sgt Percy J. McFadden
Capt Buell A. Bankston
Capt Arthur P. Vandergrift
2Lt Lawrence H. Kiskaddon
2Lt Thomas M. Poole
S/Sgt Ralph V. Metcalf
S/Sgt Lee J. Cobb
T/Sgt Alfred Lefevre
1Lt Joseph Robert Janovsky
2Lt Clair Elwood Lewis
S/Sgt Henry B. Evans
S/Sgt Edward A. Witt
S/Sgt Howard Ferguson

2Lt Paul M. Pitts	2Lt Donald L. Knapp
2Lt William C. McClure	S/Sgt Ralph Powell
2Lt George R. Beninga	Sgt Henry E. Brown
2Lt Hillary S. Blackwell	S/Sgt Donald W. Austin
Cpl Peter J. Biscan	Sgt. Horace S. Bowen Jr.
S/Sgt Robert F. Deutsch	S/Sgt Danial Hall
2Lt Marshall S. Hawke	2Lt Michael Rusnak
1Lt Clifford O. Sherry	2Lt Morse A. Nielson
2Lt John E. Hancock	2Lt Gilbert P. Johnson
2Lt Harold L. Feinauer	Sgt Joseph C. Redman
Sgt George W. Rhine	2Lt Thomas F. Neal
2Lt Wellington W. Kennison	1Lt Logan W. Hughes
2Lt Rufus S. Humphries Jr.	LT N.S. Lynn
2Lt Haig P. Wylie	Sgt J.M. Williams
2Lt Frank J. Moore	Cpl G.E. Fry
S/Sgt Joseph E. Messina	2nd Lt Lloyd J. Porsch
S/Sgt Stanley F. Warshak	2Lt Lloyd Porsch
S/Sgt Horace C. Holt	2Lt Rollin N. Wilson Jr.
2Lt James W. Peterson	2Lt Thomas C. Bodkin Jr.
2Lt Henry H. Hoffman	2Lt Harris S. Haywood
2Lt Robert M. Reser	Sgt Herbert Furhman
2Lt Thomas H. Fail	Sgt Frank J. Hamman
S/Sgt William W. Colby	2Lt John Bacsik Jr.
S/Sgt Joseph T. Dervan	2Lt Alfred M. Hebert
Sgt James S. Welch	2Lt Ford F. Simmonds
1Lt Leslie W. Shepard	2Lt Morris P. Davis
2Lt Thomas C. Galbraith	2Lt Edward E. Pennell
2Lt Warren E. Smith	2Lt Harold W. Follmer
T/Sgt Weldon E. Boone	2Lt David B. Edge Jr.
T/Sgt Bill G. Comerford	2Lt Phelps Miller Jr.
Sgt Walter J. Szychulski	2Lt Richard B. Wright
Cpl Harold F. Lamieux	Sgt Henry R. Stables
1Lt Floyd C. Grazier Jr.	Sgt John R. Collins Jr.
2Lt John G. Schuten	Capt Hugh F. Lister
2Lt Howard H. Dailey	Pvt John R. Darby
2Lt William L. Price	S/Sgt Glen A. Edwards
2Lt Eugene W. Feldott	2Lt James T. Ramsey
2Lt Matt A. Pansky	2Lt Robert Kohn
2Lt Rodney F. Russell	2Lt James E. Lasseter

2Lt Charles E. Sutton
Sgt Timothy M. Moody
Cpl Warren C. Collins
S/Sgt Herbert A. Newton
2Lt James McCallum
Sgt Dean L. Morrison
1Lt James R. Derflinger
F/O Joseph Price Kelley
Sgt Thomas P. Fitzsimmons
WASP Susan Parker Clark
2Lt Harry C. Thomas
2Lt Marvin A. Wolf
2Lt Richard H. Bell
2Lt George E. Cisco
2Lt Yarslav Naveschuk
Cpl Arthur Henry Stedman
Cpl David Benjamin Mermell
Cpl Paul Convey Smith
Capt R.W. Miller
2Lt R.R. Coates
2Lt D.C. Estes

2Lt W.R. McDermott
Cpl J.A. Dacek
Cpl L.R. DuBreevil
Pfc G.L. Simms
Pfc O.R. Rhodes
Sgt T.C. Conway
F/O Robert M. Johnson
2Lt E.C. Knowlton
Cpl L.T. DuGovic
Pfc H.D. Sidman
2Lt Cornelieus D. Dowling
2Lt Edward Powell
2Lt Everett Edward Thompson
Cpl William Henry Strong
Cpl Edmund Robert Utne
F/O Robert B. Tuskey
F/O Donald D. Crosby
Cpl Robert Hanneman
Cpl Robert B. Bogdewiecz
S/Sgt Herbert A. Newton
2Lt Willis E. Moore

ABOUT THE AUTHOR AND DESIGNER

Rachel Haynie

Rachel Haynie realized when she was researching and writing **Stalled**, her first book, there was no history – longer than a few pages – on Columbia Army Air Base. Stalled is historical fiction also set in and around Columbia Army Air Base. With the approaching 70th anniversary of Columbia Army Air Base, she felt the base's importance to local and area history warranted a history, so began the task. She also is author of **Myths and Mysteries of South Carolina**, published by Globe Pequot Press, and **First, You Explore**, a juvenile biography on South Carolina Nobel Laureate and laser pioneer Dr. Charles Townes. Haynie is a graduate of the University of South Carolina. Info.caab@gmail.com.

Pat Saad

Pat Saad, a fine artist and a most versatile designer, has created corporate logos, brochures, collateral materials, newsletters and magazines, as well as jewelry, now collected by discerning women throughout the region. She was the designer on Rachel Haynie's first book, entitled **Stalled**. Saad is a graduate of the University of South Carolina.

Made in the USA
Charleston, SC
15 May 2012